LICENSE TO DREAM

EVERY WOMAN'S DREAM TO FINANCIAL FREEDOM THROUGH NETWORK MARKETING

SECOND EDITION

Judy O'Higgins

Kristi Lee

Karen Palmer

License to Dream: Every Woman's Guide to Financial
Freedom Through Network Marketing,
Second Edition

©2023, 2010 Judy O'Higgins, Kristi Lee, Karen Palmer.

First Edition Published and distributed in the United States by
The Network Marketing Dream Team.

Second Edition: Published by New Frontier Books, LLC
Edited by Holly Doherty.

Photography by Rafy Ruiz.

The hypothetical examples set forth in this book are intended
to explain elements of network marketing. These examples
are not representative of the income, if any, that an independent distributor can or will earn, and any figures used are
not a representation of earnings you should anticipate. Simi-
larly, any downline growth examples presented show a
downline organization growing in a symmetrical fashion.
This is for purposes of illustration only; in reality, organizations do not grow fully or symmetrically. Success with a network marketing business results only from successful sales efforts, which require effort, diligence, and leadership. Your
success will depend on how effectively you exercise these
qualities.

ISBN: 9798377308096

To Kody Bateman, thank you for dreaming big and never giving up on your dreams. We share the same dream of changing the world. You gave me the vehicle to do it, and my life will never be the same.

Judy O'Higgins

To my Heavenly Father, thank you for putting a huge vision in my heart and giving me the gifts and talents to inspire people. To my daughter, Jade, you are my biggest "why" and I am incredibly blessed to be your mom. To my mother, Rose, thank you for your unwavering support and your belief that I can achieve anything. To my BBB Cousin, thank you for always walking through fire with me and having enough faith for both of us when I needed it. To women everywhere, may you be true to yourself and have the courage to step into your greatness...together we can change the world.

Kristi Lee

To my family whose love and support I know I can always count on... may you always have the courage to dream big!

Karen Palmer

CONTENTS

INTRODUCTION
OUR DREAMS

Do you remember the dreams you had as a little girl? Did you want to be a lawyer? A teacher? A CEO? A mom? An astronaut? An author? A movie star? As a child, we believe we can do and be anything. But, somewhere along the way, we seem to lose that wonder of childhood. We forget what it means to dream big—or to dream at all.

Do you find yourself lying awake in bed worrying about losing your job? Have you already lost your job and searched in vain for a new one? Do you wish you could find a way to create a better future for yourself and your family? Instead of dreaming, are you worrying?

Maybe you are a Baby Boomer or nearing retirement. Data from the Insured Retirement Institute notes that 45% of Baby Boomers surveyed had no savings. Do you feel unprepared for retirement? Whether you are on a fixed income, like social security, or your 401(k) looks insufficient due to inflation, you might be one of the millions thinking that you will need to postpone retirement because they are afraid they can't afford to stop working. Is this you?

Maybe you are still young but stressed out and working insane hours at your job. Are you depressed over being unable to spend quality time with your spouse and children? Do you feel the pain of missing out on the important events in your children's lives? Maybe you are rethinking how to earn income because of the uncertainties in our world today, like the recession of 2008 or the pandemic of 2020. As millions of people transitioned to work from home in 2020, they discovered incredible benefits, like spending quality time with their family and pets, enjoying more flexibility, having no commute (and spending less on gas and maintenance), and even working in their pajamas!

Have you lost your dreams for your future, or do you see them fading away?

Are you willing to think outside the box to get your dreams back?

Are you ready for a change?

If you answered yes, you have come to the right place! Our goal for this book is to give you back your life's dreams and provide the tools to make them come true.

It's time to stop waiting to retire, to stop waiting until your kids grow up, to stop waiting for "someday" to arrive. It's time to stop putting the true desires of your heart on hold.

Our desire is to empower you to recapture your dreams and, more than that, to pursue and manifest them. Not later...now!

WHO ARE WE?

We are three women representing diverse age groups, from Baby Boomer to a mom with kids at home, who decided NOT to place our lives on hold any longer. Through the magic of network marketing, we are moving toward the freedom we've always dreamed of—that all of us dream of. Although we are in different stages of life and in different stages of our journey toward financial freedom, we have all given ourselves a license to dream big—to allow ourselves to conceive of the formerly impossible as possible.

In this book, we'll show you how we are achieving our dreams by thinking "outside the box" and using a simple concept to create financial freedom, time freedom, and lifestyle freedom. Here is a snapshot of the freedoms we have achieved and want to help you reach, too.

JUDY *(RETIRED BABY BOOMER)*

Judy wakes up when she wants to, plays with her dog Boomer, and takes the thirty-second commute to her home office in her pajamas. She works when she chooses and has no boss telling her when to go to lunch. She never has to ask for a vacation; she just books a flight and hops on a plane.

Judy is her own boss and has total control over her choices. She can meet a friend for coffee any day of the week, catch a movie matinee, or take a cruise to Alaska at a moment's notice. She hasn't had to live by a nine-to-five routine in years. After just two years with her home-based business, she matched her income from her twenty-five-year career as a counselor and retired!

Judy receives automatic deposits in her bank account almost daily! Her retirement is funded for the rest of her life—regardless of what happens to the stock market, Social Security, or the economy. She is grateful every day for the blessings of financial security and knowing she will never have to get a part-time job to help with the rent or to pay her bills.

KRISTI *(CORPORATE AMERICA SURVIVOR)*

Kristi is able to set her own schedule each day since she left corporate America. She was able to go on every school field trip with her daughter, volunteer in her daughter's classroom, and spearhead projects like raising thousands of dollars for her daughter's Girl Scout troop selling Girl Scout cookies without worrying about it interfering with a job. Now that her daughter is in college, she is available to support her.

She attends seminars and events without having to ask a boss for permission. She will never be told to relocate her family one more time since resigning from the corporate rat race and becoming her own boss with her own home-based business.

Now Kristi is putting her training and marketing talents to work for herself and her own business team, instead of making someone else in corporate America wealthy. She sets her own business schedule, works the hours she chooses, and feels grateful for the freedom and security of being in control of her own life. She is on her way to financial freedom and lifestyle freedom!

KAREN *(COLLEGE PROFESSOR AND MOM OF FOUR)*

When Karen first started her business, she had three small children at home. Her business enabled her to choose her projects and deadlines. When it rained outside, she could take time with her kids to bake chocolate chip cookies and make hot cocoa. On sunny afternoons, she could take time off to sit on the porch and eat Popsicles. She could choose to put her family first.

Now, as a full-time college professor, Karen often has to schedule her family around her job. However, Karen's business still enables her to have flexibility. She and her husband take time to play with their kids. When they go on business trips, they make it a family vacation.

They get out of their home-based business what they put in, and that time and effort are leveraged as their business grows. They look forward to a life of complete financial freedom—no debt, no worries about paying bills on time or using the credit card to buy groceries, and no fear of losing their home.

Even though each of us has a different lifestyle, we each receive money in our bank accounts regularly, which allows us time and lifestyle freedom. How did we achieve this? How can YOU?

THE ANSWER IS RESIDUAL INCOME.

This book is a roadmap that guides you step-by-step through how to achieve the same results. We invite you to leave behind your self-doubt, skepticism, and old ways of thinking. Pick up the roadmap in this book, follow the steps we have detailed for you in the following chapters, and give yourself a license to dream again. Join us and thousands of others on the road to financial freedom. It's all here for you if you are ready!

KEY POINT

NOTE: We have used an analogy of driving a car and taking a trip to describe what it is like for a woman who is unfamiliar with network marketing to gain a better understanding, not only of the profession but also herself. Throughout the book, you will find key facts (denoted with the "Key Point" graphic like the one shown here) that we believe are significant in building a successful business. These facts have helped us shorten our learning curve and increase our earning curve!

Cherish your visions and your dreams, as they are the children of your soul, the blueprints of your ultimate achievements.

—NAPOLEON HILL

CHAPTER 1
THE SUPERHIGHWAY TO FINANCIAL FREEDOM

I f you're like most women, you've probably spent a lot of time thinking about what needs to happen for you to achieve your dreams. Have you fantasized about winning the lottery? Getting a surprise inheritance? Marrying rich?

There's a better way—one that is totally within your control. What if there was a way to get paid over and over again, just for telling people about an amazing product or service that you already use and love?

THE MAGIC OF RESIDUAL INCOME

If you are new to the concept and the power of residual income, here's a brief explanation. Most of us are familiar with the idea that, once a song is recorded, the artist gets a small amount of money every time that song airs on radio or TV and every time someone buys it. An artist can record a song once and receive ongoing royalty income, as many people listen to it for years to come. THAT is residual income—and it's why Elvis makes more money now than when he was alive!

Here's another example. When you buy a book on Amazon, the author receives a small amount of money for that sale. It's not much by itself. The power is in many people buying it over time, creating a monthly revenue stream for the author for something she did one time (writing the book).

THAT is residual income.

If you're not a gifted writer or singer, you can still create this kind of ongoing income and benefit from it for life. We know because we have done it, and SO CAN YOU! Here's how…

Have you ever gone to a great movie or a restaurant that you loved and then told your family, co-workers, and friends about it? What if you had money deposited in your bank account every time one of those people (which we call your "network") went to the movie or ate at the restaurant? What if you recommended that movie or restaurant to fifty people, and forty of them went? If your referral bonus was $10 per person, you would receive checks totaling $400 just for telling people you know about the movie or restaurant. If you did the same thing the next month, you would receive another check for $400.

What could you do with an extra $400 a month?

NETWORK MARKETING

In today's world, the typical consumer is overly bombarded with advertising on TV, radio, internet, print, and all of our devices! Traditional advertising and marketing have become less and less effective in this information age, because we have learned to tune it out just to survive.

However, the "old-fashioned" concept of one person recommending a product or service they love to others is alive and well. The personal recommendation is even MORE powerful in today's society—where impersonal technology rules—because it comes from a trusted source.

Many companies have come to this conclusion and are using an alternative business model called network marketing, or affiliate marketing, to get the word out about their products and services. There are thousands of companies using the network marketing model today, because word-of-mouth advertising is more effective than ever.

The basis of this model is the simple concept that if someone loves a product or service and tells others about it, she deserves to be financially rewarded by the company that makes the product or provides the service when her referrals purchase it.

Have you ever caught yourself saying, "I wish I had a dollar for every time I told someone about..."? Well, now you can, and those dollars can add up fast!

Going back to the example of getting paid for recommending a movie or restaurant: What if you got paid AGAIN every time those forty people went back to eat at that restaurant for life?

THAT is residual income—getting paid over and over for something you did one time! And that is how Judy got to retire, Kristi got to leave corporate America, and Karen got to stay home with her kids.

MORE MAGIC: LEVERAGED INCOME

Let's take our example one step further. What if you got paid AGAIN when the people who ate in the restaurant you recommended told THEIR friends, family, and co-workers, who also ate there? How about getting paid yet AGAIN when those people tell THEIR network of friends, family, and associates, who also then visit the restaurant? And then AGAIN when this group repeats the process?

Repeat this scenario several more times. Now you can imagine how you could receive substantial income for something you started—but which then took on a life of its own without you—and get paid over and over, every time someone buys a product or service that you or someone in your network recommends!

There are many thousands of people successfully doing just that to pay their mortgages, finance their retirements, raise their families, send their children to college, and escape the corporate rat race. Thousands of ordinary women (like the three of us) with no special education or previous skills are creating the kind of income that can bring their dreams back to life and sustain them with a lifestyle many would not believe possible. If you want to be one of them, this book will show you how we are doing it and what you must do to get the same results.

THE BUSINESS MODEL FOR TODAY'S ECONOMY

Robert Kiyosaki is one of the most respected and successful business writers and entrepreneurs of our time. In his book, The Business of the 21st Century, Kiyosaki heartily endorses network marketing as the best business model for the average woman to create her own wealth in today's economy. He correctly points out that the old success model of getting a good job and sticking with it for years is over.

Respected financial advisor Dave Ramsey often reminds us that an expensive college education is no longer a guarantee of a good job. Experts like Kiyosaki and Ramsey urge us to let go of our old ideas about how to build economic security for our families and to embrace entrepreneurial models for achieving our dreams. They urge us all to take control of our financial destinies by becoming entrepreneurs.

For those who want to follow their advice, the time is NOW to start a business that can take you down the road to financial freedom, lifestyle freedom, and TRUE security for yourself and your family.

TOP 10 BENEFITS OF NETWORK MARKETING

Below is a summary of the many benefits of network marketing that make it what we believe to be the best choice for you if you don't want to keep trading time for money in your job, don't want to keep working forever, and don't want the headaches and financial risk of a traditional business or franchise.

1. YOU'RE THE BOSS.
When you decide to share a company's products or services for profit, you are an independent contractor, not an employee. This means you have no boss, no supervisor, and no one to answer to but yourself. You do get guidance and help from the company, as well as from the person who introduced you to the company, but without the downside of having to report to a boss as in the traditional business model. YOU are truly your own boss and in charge of your financial destiny.

2. FORGET THE NINE-TO-FIVE ROUTINE.
You can focus as few or as many hours each week as you choose to put into your home business, and you choose which hours. You also have no employees to manage, like you would in a franchise model or traditional business. You have total freedom to run your business in the way that works best for your lifestyle.

Most people in network marketing work only part time, yet it is possible to replace your full-time job income in just a few years of part-time effort with the network marketing model. The flexibility of working hours is also a great benefit to women who choose to stay at home with their children. Imagine working your home business around your children's nap times like Karen did.

3. AVOID THE COMMUTE TO AN OFFICE.

You can operate out of your home office or from your dining room table. With the current fluctuation in gas prices, the commute from your bedroom to your home office is a huge benefit. Most of us just need a phone, a computer, and high-speed internet access. The simplicity of the network marketing business model is a benefit that cannot be overemphasized.

4. REDUCE YOUR TAXES.

With a home business, you can write off the cost of a phone, a computer, and high-speed internet, among other things. You can also get reimbursed for every mile you drive that you can attribute to your home business. Other deductions may include a percentage of your utility bills (depending on what percentage of your home is taken up by your home office), uninsured health care expenses, equipment such as a printer, and more. (Consult your accountant or financial advisor.) The tax breaks for home-based businesses are some of the best in America today, and this alone can save the average taxpayer thousands a year.

5. ENJOY LOW START-UP COSTS.

There are well over 1,000 companies today using the network marketing business model to spread the word about their products. Why? Because it works. Word- of-mouth recommendations for a product or service are much more powerful than advertising. In most cases, the start-up cost to get your business going ranges from only $25 to $500. A person can get started for under $1,000, in contrast to franchise and traditional business models, where start-up costs typically run many thousands of dollars.

You can see one big reason this type of business is so attractive, especially in our current economy. The risk and upfront investment are minimal. And don't forget that, unlike the other business models, you can work this type of business part time around your lifestyle, or full time for faster results. Either way, it beats shelling out $50,000 to $500,000 or more for a franchise or traditional business—assuming you could even get a loan for one in today's economy!

6. REALIZE HIGH REWARD POTENTIAL.

The network marketing model offers average people the chance to make excellent income with no limits imposed by a corporate salary structure. There is also no glass ceiling to limit the advancement of women. Everyone starts with a level playing field and has the same potential for success. Promotions are based solely on your efforts, not the whims of your boss.

Remember that in the franchise and traditional business models, it typically takes years to break even before you see a profit. With the network marketing model, you can be profitable after just a few weeks—and go on to replace your job income (and beyond) to achieve your financial goals and dreams. There are no limits to what you can achieve!

7. RECEIVE CHECKS WITH COMMAS (RESIDUAL INCOME).

After a relatively short time (usually months, not years) of consistent work with a network marketing business, entrepreneurs can receive residual income based on your own efforts. Doesn't relying on your own efforts beat the heck out of relying on something out of your control, especially in a world of uncertainty?

As long as your product users keep buying and using the product you recommended, you will continue to receive income automatically, like singers who continue to get royalties from songs they recorded years ago. This ability to receive monthly passive residual income over and over from a sale you made one time is a key component of what truly sets network marketing apart from other business models.

After a few years of building this type of business through your own efforts, it can be possible to do whatever you want, like take a world cruise or travel the country while passive income continues to come in. On the other hand, if you should you become ill or face any other unforeseen circumstances, the monthly income still keeps coming in like clockwork!

This is the meaning of TRUE financial security and freedom—not being dependent on corporate America, the government, or any other entity for your financial health.

8. LEVERAGE YOURSELF.

Financial experts say you must leverage yourself to create true wealth, and the network marketing model does just that. Here's how it works:

- You find a product you love and start using it.
- You recommend it to a few others, who also start using it. You get paid for each one.
- Some of them also want an income from recommending the product to others they know. For each person who follows your lead and duplicates what

you are doing, you can earn a percentage of every-thing they and THEIR customers buy each month.

- This repetition continues down a line of people for several levels through the process of duplication, and your checks start growing. You get paid on eve-rything that is transacted by your team, as well as on your own efforts.
- Imagine that as your team grows, you start earning income for what the newer people do—people you may not even know. Your team could expand to several states, and possibly other countries!

9. LEVERAGE YOUR TIME.

In the "job world," you can only work so many hours, and your income is limited by that reality. Even a second job only adds so much income before you are at your limit.

In the network marketing world, the hours you work can be duplicated by your team. If you work five hours a week in your home business, and you have ten people on your team who also work five hours each, that is fifty hours of productivity in a week—plus your own five hours. Can your job do that?

10. EXPERIENCE PERSONAL GROWTH.

Network marketing has been described as a personal growth program with a compensation plan attached. You will learn new skills. You will surround yourself with pos-itive messages and people. To be successful, you will focus on creating and maintaining a positive attitude and mind-set.

In a world where everything we hear is ninety percent negative, you will become a beacon of hope to those who come into your business and your life. You will have the satisfaction of mentoring and helping many others to im-prove their lives as well.

You will grow in self-confidence and ultimately do things you never thought you could. Judy never imagined that she would be on stage speaking to large groups, but she has done exactly that many times!

Does all of this sound too good to be true? Trust us, it's not. People all over the world use the magic of network marketing to enable them to dream again. We are doing it, and so can you. And there has never been a better time than right now—today!

THINK IT OVER...

- What are some of the dreams you have put aside? What are some challenges you are facing now?
- How could network marketing and residual income help you get your dreams back? How could it help you overcome your current challenges?
- What are you most excited about after reading this chapter?
- What questions do you still have?

CHAPTER 2
CHOOSE YOUR VEHICLE

If you have made the decision to join us on the road trip to financial freedom with network marketing and get that residual income stream started, congratulations! Before you jump in with both feet, here are some tips about choosing the right company that can keep you motivated as you build your business, while others fail before they get started.

BELIEVE IN YOUR PRODUCT AND COMPANY.

Your network marketing "career" will likely require several years of working part time to replace your job income and several more years to achieve true financial freedom and generational wealth, depending on your goals and how fast you choose to build your business. Since you will be sharing a product or service for that length of time as you build to the income of your dreams, it is CRITICAL that you really love and believe in your product and its value. If not, you will lack the passion that attracts others to you like a magnet.

Here's the key: Would you use, love, and recommend the product(s) to others, whether or not you were getting paid?

If the answer is no, then do not sign up with that company! The importance of this principle cannot be overstated. Many people get started with the first company they hear about, instead of doing their homework and choosing a product/service they truly feel passionate about. If you pick a company randomly and only do it for the money, your road could be long and bumpy.

THE PRODUCT

If you know and believe in your heart that your product or service can absolutely benefit every person's life with whom you share it, your path will be much easier. You will achieve your goals and dreams more quickly because of the positive energy you send out to the world and your passion for helping others with the product. So, choose wisely!

Here are some practical questions to ask yourself when considering potential products:

1. IS SOMETHING SIMILAR IN QUALITY OR PRICE OFFERED IN STORES LIKE WAL-MART OR AMAZON?

Be prepared to compete with those types of retail stores if your potential product line includes widely distributed products.

2. DO OTHER NETWORK MARKETING COMPANIES OFFER A SIMILAR PRODUCT OR SERVICE?

Remember, your potential customer can be confused by several people telling them, "Ours is the best."

The ideal product/service to align yourself with:

- has little or no competition or stands out from the crowd
- is not subject to whims of government regulatory groups like the FDA or FTC
- is easy to use
- solves a common problem
- has potential for high physical or emotional positive impact

3. WHAT MODEL DOES THE COMPANY USE FOR SHARING ITS PRODUCTS? DOES THAT MODEL FIT WITH YOUR PERSONALITY AND LIFESTYLE?

If you love cosmetics, skin care, jewelry, or women's clothing and love to entertain, your ideal company could be one that sells these products and uses the home party model to spread the word.

Do you love to cook? There are companies that will pay you for demonstrating and recommending cookware and kitchen products.

If you are passionate about healthy living and want to grow your income by helping others become healthier, consider companies that feature vitamins, air and water filters, essential oils, fitness and weight loss, and other health-oriented products.

If you would prefer a service so you don't have to deal with inventory, returns, and cost of samples and shipping, consider companies that offer legal services, communications, or internet-based greeting cards.

The good news is that, thanks to services like Zoom and Facebook Live, anyone can share their products from home, while on vacation, or anywhere!

4. WHAT ARE THE AFFILIATE PURCHASING REQUIREMENTS?

All companies that use the network marketing model ask their representatives to buy and use their product/service themselves. After all, how can you recommend something you have no personal experience with? This is another important reason to LOVE your product/service, as you will be a "product of your product" for your career with the company.

There can be a wide variation in the monthly cost, depending on how expensive your product/service is. Again, do your homework and ask questions to gain awareness of your potential company's requirements before you join them as an independent representative.

THE COMPANY

After you have chosen the type of product or service, the next important step is to evaluate the company itself and, more importantly, its leadership. You can have the world's greatest product, but if the company is mismanaged or the leadership is not sharp, passionate about their product, and in it for the long term—or if they do not understand how to work with the network marketing model—the company will probably not last.

Do some research on your potential choice. Meet the founders and CEO if you can. Otherwise, join a live stream or watch a video presentation. Pay close attention to the energy they bring to the event, as well as their actions and words.

- Do they have a big vision for the company?
- What is the "culture" or philosophy of the company? Is it all about making money, or do they have a vision for making the world a better place?
- Are they passionate about their product?
- Do they put the needs of their independent representatives at the top of their priority list?
- Do they have shareholders to answer to? (Remember, their decisions will directly affect you.)
- Do they have a solid and well-conceived plan for the company's future growth?
- What is the company's debt situation?
- Is the product elaborate and expensive to produce? The higher the cost of creating the products, the more expensive and less competitive they will be. If you can, tour the home office to see how the product is made.
- Do the customer service reps or home office employees seem happy and eager to help? Is it a hassle to get through to customer service, or it is a pleasant experience? Remember, these folks will be your future customer service reps, handling the people you refer to buy your product/service.

THE BOTTOM LINE

You want a CEO and a leadership team who are totally committed to the company long term and who have a personal passion for how the product/service can help people.

The CEO is not just there for the adventure of starting and growing a company and then selling it. He/she should have a big vision and dreams of making a difference.

Your future success in network marketing depends on a company whose leaders have the heart and commitment to make wise choices and place your interest as a representative at the top of their priority list. You are about to choose the vehicle to take you down the road to financial freedom, so choose wisely!

THINK IT OVER...

Often, we are introduced to network marketing by a friend or family member. We might decide to join them because we like that person or get caught up in their excitement, or maybe even because we feel obligated. It's important to do some research and make sure the company is actually a good fit for you before getting started.

Here are some questions to ask yourself when choosing a network marketing company:

1. What are some of the products or services you currently use? What do you like/not like about the companies you purchase from?

2. What are some other categories of products/services you might be interested in? The following websites include a list of all of the network marketing companies around the world. Jot down a list of five to ten companies that pique your interest.
- https://laconteconsulting.com/mlm-direct-sales-global-list/
- https://www.dsa.org/

3. What type of sharing would you be most comfortable with? Home party? Demonstrations? Social media sharing? One on one?

4. Just like sharing your favorite restaurant or movie, can you get excited about sharing the product or service with others?

CHAPTER 3
SET YOUR INTERNAL GPS

U p to this point, we have focused on the importance of belief in the network marketing business model, the product, and the company. There is, however, one more area of belief that is even more important: belief in YOURSELF!

KEY POINT

The most important key to success in your network marketing business is inside yourself!

The secret to success in network marketing has been called many things, including "mindset" and the "inner game." However you name it, it is composed of two things, both hugely important.

HAVE A BIG DREAM—YOUR WHY.

Now is the time to retrieve your dreams from the back of the closet, dust them off, and make them shine again. What is your goal or Big Dream of how you want your life to look at the end of your network marketing career? Your dream can be whatever you choose, but it should be BIG, and definitely bigger than you—involving others who become part of your vision and help you carry it out.

Your Big Dream could involve making the world a better place because of your products/services or funding a nonprofit with the proceeds. For example, your dream might involve others in the following ways:

- helping people with their health issues
- helping people raise their self-esteem
- setting up a nonprofit foundation
- helping children around the world
- funding an animal rescue organization

Your Big Dream should include your family, helping them have a better life by sharing in your financial success. Examples could include:

- retiring your hard-working spouse from his/her job
- financing your children's college education
- setting up a trust fund for your grandchildren
- traveling or going on vacations with your family
- buying a vacation home or an RV

Another word for your Big Dream is your "WHY." Your *why* is your reason for making a commitment to start a new business, learn new skills, put in consistent hours for a few years, and overcome the inevitable bumps in the road—and even some detours—on the highway to financial freedom. Your why has to be big enough and strong enough to handle any temporary setback that is put in your path—every obstacle and all forms of negativity, both internal and external, that threaten to derail your dream. Make it big!

JUDY'S BIG DREAM

Inspire millions of baby boomers to achieve financial freedom and live their retirement dreams through the principles and action steps outlined in this book. As my company expands internationally, get paid to spread our model of financial freedom to women worldwide.

KRISTI'S BIG DREAM

Empower and inspire women around the planet financially, emotionally, and spiritually, so they can teach their children to do the same. Empower and inspire people in the corporate world to reclaim their lives and create generational wealth for their family and future generations.

KAREN'S BIG DREAM

Empower women, especially moms, to embrace their desires to be present in their homes while still pursuing their passions and utilizing their gifts to help others. Be completely financially free and enjoy the freedom to put my family first. Support the ministries that are near and dear to my heart.

HERE'S A TIP TO HELP YOU:

Before you get started, make a vision board with visual reminders of your why. You can download an app to create a vision board, but there is something very powerful about the old-fashioned process of creating a physical board, especially if you have children.

You can purchase poster board or foam board from any craft or office supply store. Cut out pictures from magazines that represent your Big Dream and what you want for yourself and your family. Paste them on the vision board.

Involve your children and spouse. Hang it in a prominent place in your home, and go back to it often to remind yourself why you are doing your business and how you will know when you are done. (Hint: Everything on the vision board will have come true!)

The bad news: You will have challenges.

The good news: You don't have to let them block you.

The best news: If your Big Dream is big enough, you will become unstoppable!

BELIEVE IN YOURSELF.

The most important thing you need to create the life of your dreams is belief in yourself. Our reality is created to a large degree by our thoughts, feelings, and belief systems. You may be holding onto negative ideas that could limit your success. If you are stuck in believing that you are a certain way and can't change or grow (for example, "I'm not a good salesperson" or "I couldn't run my own business" or "I just don't have the right personality") then you are allowing fear-based, negative thoughts to keep you from using your talents and abilities to reach your dreams and find your own greatness.

Your biggest enemy is the committee of negative voices inside your head (what your family members, teachers, and others have told you). They are just a bunch of fear-based losers whose only job is to keep you stuck in your current comfort zone of the familiar and keep you from the risk of failure that comes when you try something new. Their voices might sound like this:

- "But you have no sales experience."
- "But you're too _____ (old, young, shy, dumb, etc.) to be a success."
- "What if you fail?"
- "What if it doesn't work?"

Here's a reality check: You are limited only by your fear of the new and unknown. What if it DOES work, and you could create financial freedom for yourself and your family? What if you missed out on your shot at your dreams because you were too afraid to try? THAT would be the only real way to fail!

You don't need experience to be successful. You will receive all the training you need from your company and the person or group that introduced you to the business. When we started out, we had no sales training and no experience.

What you DO need:

- products/services you love
- desire to share them
- passion to help others
- basic company training and education from your team leaders about how to succeed
- willingness to grow and step out of the traditional ways of thinking and being that may have limited you in the past

Every one of us has the capability of being successful, helping many others along the way, and making a tremendous contribution to the world. Don't allow the committee to steal your dream! Take the first steps and have faith in yourself and all you are capable of. Your greatness will begin to unfold as the path to your dreams appears beneath your feet, one step at a time. You will have many people to help and guide you along the way, and you will grow in ways you can't even imagine.

Network marketing is a wonderful and rewarding venture that can change your life and the lives of your family forever.

BELIEVE that you can do it and be successful— because YOU CAN!

DETOUR—WOMEN ONLY

Belief in yourself is so important to success in network marketing and in life. Because many women struggle with issues related to self-esteem and self-worth, we will focus briefly on issues that are especially likely to affect women. Some are cultural—a result of society's norms and gender roles, even in these modern times. Most are a result of how we were raised and the messages we still receive about "how to be" in the world.

If you do not relate to any of the examples, feel free to skip this section. If you do relate to one or more of the stories, we encourage you to not let the issue block your progress, either personally or in your business. Through your own conscious effort and support from others, you can overcome any limiting beliefs from your past. Your network marketing business can be your vehicle to personal transformation, helping you overcome anything that is keeping you from fully participating in life's abundance.

You deserve it. Don't let anything hold you back!

JUDY'S STORY

In my own experience, including my twenty-five years of being a women's counselor, I have seen so many women (especially of my Baby Boomer generation, but not limited to that age range) who grew up feeling their needs always came last on the list. We were told it was a good thing to go to college and prepare for a career. Yet in the same breath, the ultimate goal was to find a "nice boy" and get married. If that marriage were to take place, it superseded any plans for a career; the husband's needs came first.

Of course, when women became mothers, the needs of their children and family came first. This would go on for twenty years or more until the last child was grown and out of the home.

I am not suggesting that this is wrong—only that as women (particularly Baby Boomer women), we have never been taught to value our own needs. I worked with hundreds of women to correct this limiting belief in my career.

Today, I see many women still struggling with their own value and the importance of their needs in running their home-based business. They feel guilty leaving their family for business trips, trainings, or meeting a prospective team member. I can assure you that men do not struggle with this issue and have no problem asserting their needs!

If you can relate to this situation, it is important to have other women in your life who believe in your right to have your own needs and who will gently confront you when you get off track or fall back into limited ways of thinking about your worth and value. This could be your best friend, a women's support group, the person who introduced you to your network marketing company (your "sponsor"), a coach, or even a counselor. The important thing is to have other women in your life who believe in your dream and your ability to achieve it—and who will gently (or not!) encourage you to go for it, helping to override the committee.

BARBARA'S STORY

Like many women, Barbara was raised to be polite. Saying no was considered rude. Being assertive and setting boundaries with others was not okay. Many women are raised with the importance of being liked, of having others approve of them to feel okay about themselves. Their self-worth comes from without instead of from within.

These limiting beliefs affect Barbara in her network marketing career, despite her success. She finds it difficult to say no. She is a hard worker and a leader, but she struggles with setting boundaries. For example, when she hosts team events and trainings in her home, people stay too long. Barbara feels unable to tell them it's time to leave. When she provides team support and training on the phone, she can't tell people when they are getting off the subject and staying on the phone too long, wasting her valuable time. Her husband doesn't like her to be away from him at night to build her business, and this causes her internal stress.

She finds it hard to establish boundaries around her time, as it might displease others. In spite of these limitations, Barbara has become a success in her company—and she is working to overcome her limiting beliefs about herself. When she does, her success will be that much greater.

KORI'S STORY

Kori and her husband are rising stars in their company, shooting into the Top 25 Affiliate List in a relatively short period of time. Yet, like many women who are part of a husband-wife team working their network marketing business together, Kori would often hang back from being in the limelight, deferring to her husband and seeing herself in his shadow.

Then she took a company-sponsored trip without him for the first time. Here is what she discovered in her own words:

"Even though my husband and I are business partners, I discovered that I was not treating him as an equal partner, but as the stronger, wiser, more informative partner. I not only looked to him for guidance, but would also direct our team members and customers to him for the more challenging questions within our business. On my trip, when I was asked the same questions that I would usually direct to my husband, the answers flowed from me like water!"

From that experience, Kori found her own voice and realized she had the same level of knowledge and skill as her husband. She made the commitment to herself to value herself equally to her husband in expertise and step into her own power and greatness. Now Kori has become an example to the other women in her business. What an incredible lesson!

JODI'S STORY

Jodi is an example of a woman who grew up with self-doubt and limiting beliefs about herself. Her internal committee told her for years, "You aren't the woman you SHOULD be."

Jodi's insecurities manifested outwardly in a quest for perfection. She needed to always have her home look perfect and her children be perfectly behaved. She tried to control everything on the outside to make up for feelings of "not good enough" on the inside. Can you imagine how hard it would be to run a successful home-based business with these thoughts?

Finally, after much internal struggle, Jodi spent one entire day mentally and emotionally letting go of her old ideas of who she should be. She released anger and tears along with her old thinking patterns. At the end of this purposeful release, Jodi was able to replace those old limiting beliefs with ones that told her, "You are okay just the way you are. Just be yourself." Jodi's world has been a much more harmonious place ever since.

Would it surprise you to know that this woman is the wife of a network marketing company CEO? This is proof that self-doubt and insecurity can affect any woman—from the CEO's wife to the brand-new distributor. Learning to let go and replace the limiting beliefs of our internal committee is the universal solution, as Jodi's story illustrates.

If you relate to any of these issues of people pleasing, perfectionism, inability to say no or set boundaries, or always putting your needs on hold for others, it is so important to reach out for help. Don't allow your dreams to be sabotaged by your old limiting beliefs!

We challenge you to use your network marketing business as your vehicle—not just for financial freedom, but also for the growth and personal empowerment that will make it all possible. You deserve it!

THINK IT OVER…

What are some of your Big Dreams?

How can your dreams help your family?

How can your dreams make the world a better place?

What are some of the limiting beliefs that hold you back?

Who can help you identify and let go of your limiting beliefs?

List some positive affirmations to help you overcome those beliefs. *(We'll give you a few to get started.)*

- I am financially free!
- I am a talented, creative woman who is attracting positive people to join me in my business!
- I am achieving my dreams!

CHAPTER 4
CREATE A ROAD MAP

GOALS ARE A PATHWAY TO YOUR DREAMS!

Many successful entrepreneurs credit the mantra "What you believe you can achieve" for their success. The image in your mind of who you are and what your future looks like draws you forward. Your dream, your vision of your future, is your why. That why keeps you focused and on course.

As important as it is to have a dream, it's also vital to chart your course by setting goals for yourself. Goals guide your actions. Affirmation without action is useless.

If you think of your dream as your final destination, your goals are the stops you'll make along the way. Goals are like a road map of your future.

Sometimes, it's not easy to keep your eyes on your goals. But if you do, you will get where you want to go. Whether you are driving, walking a balance beam, or working toward your why, you have to stay focused on where you are going.

Let's say that you are planning a road trip from San Diego to New York. Would you simply dream of New York, visualize yourself there, and magically open your eyes to find yourself on Fifth Avenue? No!

While you need to know where you're going, you also have to chart a course to get there. Do you want to take the scenic route? The quickest route? Go by foot, car, train, or air? Who will you bring with you? What will you bring with you? How long do you want the trip to take?

Obviously, answering these questions ahead of time will make your trip a much more enjoyable experience, as well as ensure that you will actually make it to your destination. Likewise, your business goals should reflect both your milestones along the way (promotions, income goals, etc.), and the actions you must take to get there.

Have you ever noticed that you can control the speed of your vehicle simply by keeping your eyes on the vehicle ahead of you? You automatically pace yourself. This is also possible in building your business. Find someone to look up to—a role model. Follow where they go, do what they do, and you will get where they are! How fast are they going? What are they achieving? Follow them to set your own pace!

MAKE GOOD PROMISES

There is a formula to follow that will help you make smart goals or promises—the acronym S.M.A.R.T.

S = SPECIFIC

Be specific about what you want to accomplish. Saying "I want to have lots of money" isn't specific enough, just as saying "I'm going across the country" isn't specific enough. Do you want to go to New York state or New York City? What hotel are you staying at? A better goal would be "I'm going to the Manhattan Club on Sixth Street in

New York City so I can visit x, y, and z!" (Hint—The x, y, and z would be your dream!)

For your business, think about your dream and choose your goals accordingly. Think about the milestones you need to achieve before you get to your dream life. What promotions do you need to achieve? How about a specific dollar amount you want to earn each month? A certain number of team members or customers? Those would be your milestones along the way.

Your food and gasoline pit stops would be your actions. How many prospecting contacts do you need to make? How many new people do you need to connect with? Set specific benchmarks for yourself and specify EXACTLY what your goals are.

As women, we tend to be too nice about saying what we want. We might agree to go to a restaurant we don't like to keep harmony in our relationships or buy a dress because someone else thinks it looks great. If you can't articulate what you want in your business, you won't get there.

Choose your own goals and state them clearly, visually and in writing!

M = MEASURABLE

If we look again at our hypothetical trip to New York, we can easily measure our journey in several ways. We can calculate how many miles the trip is, how many days it will take to travel, and how much money it will cost. At any point along the way, we can easily measure our progress. We can keep track of our mileage, our time, and our expenses to see how far we've come and how we are progressing toward our destination.

In terms of your business, you can measure how many team members and customers you need to get your first promotion. You can then take a step back at any time and measure your progress. If you need to earn x amount of dollars each month, you can easily track how close you are to achieving your goal.

Are you afraid to weigh yourself because you might not like what you see? Sometimes we have to face up to our failures in order to overcome them. Creating measurable goals helps us do that. And, you never know... maybe you've gone farther than you thought!

A = ATTAINABLE

The third characteristic of a good goal is that it's attainable. A road trip to New York from San Diego is certainly attainable, as is your success in your network marketing career. However, neither goal is attainable OVERNIGHT. The farther away your dream is from your current location, the more intermediate stops you want to plan, because setting unattainable goals only sets you up for disappointment.

Your dream might be to get to the highest level in the company. However, that's not something you can achieve in one day. Some of your progress might depend on your own efforts, while other parts may depend on teaching and training your team.

A more attainable goal would be achieving your first promotion. Maybe you want to give yourself six months to get there. That is a very specific, measurable, AND attainable goal. Find out what it takes to get the first promotion, and set that as your goal.

Setting unattainable goals makes us feel like we've failed, and many people give up instead of reevaluating their goals. If you find that you've overreached, that's okay. Just take a step back and readjust. Remember that your highest dreams are possible, and to get there, you need to take the first step.

R = REALISTIC

Just as you need to choose goals that are attainable, you also want to choose goals that are realistic. Maybe you only have one hour a day to travel to New York. Is it realistic to say you will get there in one day? Of course not. You know yourself and what you can do. While you should always try to stretch yourself, you also want to be realistic about what you can accomplish within a certain time frame.

If you can only talk to one person a week, it may not be realistic to get to your first promotion in six months. Maybe it will take you a year. That's okay. It's better to set a realistic goal than one that looks good. In fact, most people in network marketing companies don't begin to see a full-time income for several years. It may take longer to get there, especially if you are new to our business model, you already have a full-time job, you are a stay-at-home mom, or you have other responsibilities. Just stick with it and remember that, most likely, it will take you a few years to get where you want to go. Remember, too, that most people overestimate what they can do in the short term, but underestimate what they can do in the long term.

Keep your dreams big and your goals realistic. That is not to say that you should hold yourself back. It's better to set your goals just a little out of reach, because you will move farther along your path if you need to push yourself a little bit.

You will rarely go past the goal you've set for yourself. In fact, we usually just get to the line. If you want to run one mile, do you ever think that you'll just run a little more once you get there, or do you slow down when the finish line is in sight?

Set realistic goals that make you stretch just a little bit.

T=TIMELINE

Goals must have a timeline. Take our trip to New York, for example. Let's say that we have a complete plan of action for getting there. We've decided on the route we want to take. We know how much it's going to cost. We know where we want to stay. But we never set a date for completing our trip.

Will we ever get there? Maybe. But our trip will be much more successful if we set our arrival date in advance.

It's the same with your business. The pace you set for yourself is determined by your timeline. So the final step is to look at your goals and set a timeline.

I HAVE MY GOALS. WHAT NOW?

Having your goals is one thing. You also have to know how to use them effectively. Otherwise, they will go in the pile with all those New Year's resolutions that are made and forgotten within a few weeks. How can you keep your goals an ongoing part of your life?

INTERNALIZE THEM

Much like you do with your dreams, you need to internalize your goals; they should become a part of you. Train your subconscious mind to move toward those goals by stating them over and over again in present tense as if they are happening right NOW. For example, "I am in New York City at the Manhattan Club on December 14, 2025."

Is this a magic formula? Maybe! Constantly feeding your mind positive affirmations that reflect your goals will have an exponential impact on your business and your quality of life. Jordan Rubin, author of The Maker's Diet, says, "In most cases, the things you do and say begin with the things you think and believe."

So imagine if, instead of telling yourself over and over, "I'm broke! I'm fat! I'm a loser!" you tell yourself, "I am earning $500 extra each month! I am healthy and fit! I am a winner!" Can you feel the difference in your attitude by just reading the statements? Imagine what could change if you made those positive statements a part of your everyday life!

SAY THEM OUT LOUD.

We believe that the power of speaking words out loud is greatly underrated. If you say your goals/affirmations out loud every day, you give the words power to act in your life. Feed yourself affirmations out loud daily as "I am" statements, and you'll find that you not only have a better outlook on life, but that you're making progress toward your goals—and ultimately your dream.

Masuru Emoto is a Japanese scientist whose belief that water is a living entity prompted him to experiment with the effect of words on water. He took samples of water and spoke words of love to one sample and words of hate to the other. Then he froze the samples. Under a microscope, the frozen water he spoke to lovingly made beautiful, symmetrical crystals. On the other hand, the water he spoke to hatefully formed twisted, ugly shapes.

As a woman, it's particularly important to beware of the words you accept into your life. Our words are not just the key to communication. They are the source of power—for good or for evil. We've all been the recipients of words that lift us up and words that bring us down. Speak only words to yourself that will lift you up—and do the same for the people in your life.

WRITE THEM DOWN

An old story says that a group of business students were interviewed about their business goals. The students were

41

grouped into three categories: those with no goals, those who simply wrote down their goals, and those who both wrote down their goals and made a clear plan for achieving them. 84% of the students had no goals at all, 13% had written their goals down, and 3% had written goals and a clear plan for achieving them. Ten years later, the students who had written down their goals were earning at least twice as much as the other students. By writing down your goals and knowing your plan for accomplishing them, you bring your dreams to life.

Everyone has heard of Jim Carrey, but you may not know about the goal he made for himself. As a struggling actor in 1987, he wrote himself a check for $10 million and dated the check for Thanksgiving 1995, with a notation that the check was for acting services rendered. Guess what? By the time the date on the check rolled around in 1995, Carrey's movies had made millions, and his price per picture was up to $20 million. That's the power of a S.M.A.R.T. goal written down!

Once you've written your goals, place them somewhere you can review them daily. We also suggest putting pictures with your goals whenever possible. Remember your vision board? This gives your mind both visual and verbal reminders of where you want to go.

FIND AN ACCOUNTABILITY PARTNER

So many of us set great goals for ourselves, but keep them a secret. Why? Just in case...just in case we fail! We might say that we'll surprise others with the results of our secret diet, but the more likely outcome is that no one will ever know we're on a diet, so we have no reason to succeed—or even try!

It is vital to find someone who you can share your goals with and who will help keep you accountable for taking the actions necessary to achieve those goals. Whether this person is a friend, a family member, or someone in your company, it is so important that you find someone to work with. Connect with them regularly to share your struggles and your successes. Together, you will help each other achieve your dreams.

As women, one of our strongest talents is the ability to network and build and nurture relationships. Take advantage of your natural desire to work together with someone, and you and your partner will help each other reach new heights.

Goals are meant to be achieved. But achieving a goal is not the end. Review your goals at least every quarter so you can adjust them according to your circumstances. If you've accomplished even one of them, great! Set your sights on the next milestone on your journey.

What if you don't achieve a goal in the timeline you set for yourself? Don't beat yourself up! Having that deadline probably pushed you to achieve more and work harder than if you hadn't set that goal.

Not meeting a goal is not a failure; it's simply not meeting a goal. If you fall down, you've got to get up and go at it again. Like a child learning to ride a bike, we have two choices: We can choose to be cynical and give up, or we can choose to be creative and move forward.

Goals are just milestones along the road to your dream. Sometimes we get there ahead of schedule, and sometimes we run a little behind. No big deal.

Sometimes there's even a detour. Don't give up! Just keep your eyes on your Big Dream, and keep checking on your progress. If you run into a challenge, chart a revised road map.

There is an old saying that the journey of a thousand miles begins with a single step. Each day we choose with our words what journey we will begin. We choose the paths our lives will take. Choose your life's direction with care. Stop saying, "I hope to someday," and make a decision today to take action and move forward to create your dream life.

THINK IT OVER...

List some goals you have already achieved.

What are some ways you can implement the concepts in this chapter?

If you are in a business already, list some S.M.A.R.T. goals.

Who is a potential accountability partner for you?

CHAPTER 5
WEAR YOUR SEATBELT – FIND SUPPORT

For women, especially, a support network is vital. We already have so much on our plates—work, family, household. With all of that going on, building a new business, no matter how important it is to you and your future, can easily fall to the wayside if you don't have the support of the people closest to you. For many people, that support will come from your family; for others, your biggest support will come from your friends or someone you've only just met in your new company.

FIND SUPPORT

As women, one of the most important reasons we decided to build a business with network marketing was our families. We wanted more time to be with them. To all of us, it is important to set our own schedules so we can enjoy time with our families and friends instead of being constantly stressed out and pushing them aside.

If you're like us, your dream or your why also has a lot to do with your family. Maybe, like Karen, you want to be involved and present in your children's lives. Maybe you want time to spend with your grandkids, your spouse, or your friends. Don't lose sight of the most important people in your life as you pursue your new business.

Without the support of the people closest to you, you may begin to lose your excitement about your dreams. If they are on board with you, then you keep each other excited. Your family can encourage you and provide a natural accountability source as you look forward to living your dreams together. Besides, it's so much more fun to do things with someone you love than to do them on your own!

INVOLVE YOUR SPOUSE

One of the best ways to involve your spouse is to dream big together. Take some time with your spouse and get away—even if it's just a walk around your neighborhood or a dinner out. Talk about what you want from life. What are your dreams? Sometimes dreams that seem impossible when they are in your head suddenly become very real when you share them with someone who is close to you.

Make sure you give your spouse time to share his dreams, too. If he can see how your new business can empower him, too, he is more likely to be supportive, if not inspired to actively help you in your business. And as soon as your first deposit shows up in your bank account, he will probably feel even more excitement and support.

When you begin your business, and every quarter as you reevaluate your progress, take time to make goals together. What do you want to accomplish and when? If you work together to formulate goals, you are more likely to achieve them. Not only are you making a verbal agreement about what you will do, but you have constant accountability through your spouse. Again, make sure that your goals take into account both of your dreams.

Building a business does take work, and it does take time. As you make your goals, think about when you want to meet those deadlines and how much time you will need.

Work together to formulate a family schedule. You'd be surprised how much time you have during the day when you sit and plan out an hourly schedule. It really is worth it! That way, you know who is doing what, and when.

Even if your spouse is not actively involved in your business, at least he will know when you are planning to work and will be better able to accommodate you. If you don't make these decisions together, you may have conflicts or confusion that could have been easily avoided simply by communicating clearly and working together.

Once you've agreed on a schedule, write it down. Or, even better, post it somewhere for everyone in the house to see. If you have small children at home, you can put up a brightly colored poster. Having a written schedule brings stability and predictability to your home, which is especially important for young children.

INVOLVE YOUR CHILDREN

Children do well when they have a predictable schedule and know what is going on in their lives. A family schedule is great for keeping your family on track, but it also helps the kids know where they are in their day. They know when they get time with their parents, what their chores are, etc. It gives them power over their day and their lives.

Here are some other benefits of including your kids in your
business:

- Allowing your kids to dream big with you also empowers them. Make your dreams a favorite family topic of conversation.
- Helping kids set goals teaches them the importance of sticking with it, managing their money, saving, etc. The list goes on and on. When Karen's daughter

47

was six, she decided she wanted an American Girl baby doll. She made a goal chart and kept track of her progress, finally earning close to $100 needed to buy her doll. At eight years old, she decided to do it again, and she bought her second American Girl doll.

- Bringing your kids with you to networking events and personal development seminars, as Kristi and Karen often do, helps them learn the importance of hard work, good listening skills, and valuable entrepreneurial skills like goal setting and networking.

While there are many opportunities to involve your children in your business, at times you will be unable to do so. If you can't afford a babysitter, don't be afraid to ask for help from family members or team members. You can even offer to trade babysitting with a team member or a family member, or pitch in on a sitter for big team events.

Remember, the goal is to build your business without neglecting your kids. Always make an effort to spend quality time with your children. You might schedule family time every evening so you can eat all of your meals together. Sit outside with your children as you check email in the afternoon and take a break to have a Popsicle or a snack.

Even sitting at a table with them while they do their homework and you work on your business creates a feeling of companionship. Sharing special little moments with your kids can make a big difference in their self-esteem and their attitudes toward you.

Given the uncertainty of the world around us, we as parents have an even greater obligation to prepare our children to have an entrepreneurial spirit so they can create their own economy as adults.

KRISTI'S STORY – PART 1

I became a single mom when my daughter Jade was three years old. My immediate family lives out of state, so it was often necessary to bring Jade to meetings. I trained her about the importance of sitting quietly through networking meetings.

Here are some tips to help your child do the same:

1. Pack a "fun bag" with age-appropriate quiet toys (puzzles, coloring books, stickers, stuffed animals).

2. Bring snacks, a drink in a spill-proof cup, and baby wipes.

3. Set your children up for success by letting them know what to expect. ("The room will look like this. There will be people on our team there. If you want to come back with me to another meeting, you will need to use your manners.")

4. Teach your child about the importance of business cards. ("This is how people will be able to call us to learn more about our business.") Business cards are never used to draw on—they mean money to our family.

5. Use positive reinforcement. ("I really like the way you are sitting quietly; you are such a big girl.")

6. Have your children use the bathroom before you leave for the meeting, and sit closest to the bathroom so you don't interrupt the meeting in case they have to go again.

7. Teach your child to look people in the eye, shake hands, and say, "Nice to meet you."

8. Do something fun, such as allowing your child to choose a reward for sitting quietly and using manners (getting an ice cream, buying a book, etc.).

9. Invite your children to be your business partners. I faced fewer objections from my daughter about meetings the minute I started calling her "my business partner" and talking to her about "our team." We kept track of our team

count on a whiteboard in our office, and Jade changed the number each time someone joined our team.

10. Teach the importance of being prepared and on time. I attended a weekly networking meeting that began at 7 a.m., before Jade's school started. I taught her how we prepared by putting our things by the door the night before (my purse and car keys, business cards, product samples, her fun bag, and her backpack). We set out clothes the night before, and I reinforced the importance of getting enough sleep. I taught her that we did this because we didn't want to be like the White Rabbit in Alice in Wonderland, who ran around saying, "I'm late, I'm late, for a very important date." As a result of this early training, Jade has become a fully functioning young adult who is totally capable of fulfilling the responsibilities of her life.

SHOW APPRECIATION

One of the most vital things we can do as women is show appreciation for our families and the people who are helping us achieve our goals. Send thank-you notes to the babysitters and family members who are supporting you. Send a card to your kids telling them how great they are. Most importantly, make sure your spouse knows how much his support means to you.

When you show your appreciation in tangible ways, people know you care about them and you aren't just using them to achieve your own goals. When people feel appreciated, they are more likely to continue supporting you.

WHAT IF YOU DON'T HAVE FAMILY?

What if you don't have family? What if your spouse isn't interested in your business? Or if you are a single mom? Find someone in your life who will support you.

Whether this someone is a friend, a family member, or someone on your team, it's vital to have an accountability partner. In fact, if you don't have a friend or family member who will support you in your goals, a team member is a perfect choice.

Share your dreams with them. Write down your goals and give them a copy so they can keep you accountable. You can work together to build a team. Go to networking events together, trade babysitting, and spend time together dreaming and making goals. Remember, your support system is vital to your success.

TAKE TIME TO BE YOU

Throughout this book, we have been using the metaphor of driving your car to your destination of financial freedom. There are many women out there—maybe even you—who are courageously taking steps toward improving themselves (going back to school, learning a skill, working outside the home, or starting a home-based business). You may experience the thrill of starting your own business. You have customers buying your product or service, and you have team members who are starting to work the business with you. Your commissions start rolling in.

As you gain confidence, your energy will start to be different, and—guess what? This changes the "script" in your personal relationships. Most of your family members and friends will be drawn to your increased vitality and self-confidence—they will want what you have.

It's important to recognize who you really are. There is a saying, "You can't move forward until you know where you've been." For you to step into your greatness, you need to be true to yourself. Find a quiet place and look inside yourself.

When was the last time you were truly happy? As women, we tend to take care of everyone else first. Many times, we never get around to taking care of ourselves. If you don't take time to refill your cup and you keep pouring yourself out to those you love and care about, you will sacrifice your sleep, your personal time, your boundaries, and your health. Much like the oxygen in an airplane, if you don't take care of yourself first, you won't be able to help anyone else.

This applies especially to building a successful network marketing business. You cannot help everyone grow their business and neglect the most important person in your life—YOU! Heal from the inside out, and all aspects of your life will get in harmony.

DETOUR: WHAT IF YOUR SPOUSE OR SIGNIFICANT OTHER IS ABUSIVE?
KRISTI'S STORY –PART 2

If you are in an abusive relationship, your spouse or significant other will recognize that your business is not a hobby. If they fear losing control over you, they may sabotage your business.

I was married for almost sixteen years. There were signs while we were dating that he had anger issues—the blow-ups, followed by apologies, and then treating me sweetly...until the next time. I chose to ignore the red flags because we had more good times than bad. And after all, he loved me, and didn't that outweigh the negative stuff?

I was successful in my career, getting promotion after promotion and overseeing people and projects. Yet my personal life was a mess.

Women will compartmentalize their personal and business lives as if they are two different people. One day, my best friend sat me down and said, "I want you to read these questions and answer them. I am going to stay right here while you do." It was a series of questions that identified being in an abusive relationship.

I looked at her and said, "I'm not in an abusive relationship. He has never hit me." But as I read the questions, I answered many more yes than no. I was sobbing by the time I got to the end. I didn't realize that abuse isn't just physical—that it can be emotional, financial, spiritual, and mental. That's not something we are taught in school, and it's certainly not something that is taught at home. It took me several more years to gain the courage and confidence to finally leave.

As our marriage was ending, so was my twenty-three-year corporate career in marketing and retail. My company was moving out of state (prompting what would have been my fourth move), and my gut feeling was that the move was just a strategy to buy time with the stockholders.

I told my husband that I wanted to start my own business, utilizing the twenty-three years of experience I had gained becoming a marketing consultant, to help companies analyze what they were doing, make suggestions, and get results.

He asked, "What is your Plan B if you fail?"

It was then I knew I had to leave this marriage, or I would never be able to spread my wings and truly soar.

At first, I resisted getting professional counseling for many reasons: I felt I could handle it on my own; it was just one more "failure" that I needed to seek help about; I would have to be vulnerable in front of a stranger.

I went through three counselors before I found one who was a good fit. He was instrumental in helping me get through this very difficult, emotional time in my life.

Just about the same time, a life coach in my BNI group taught a Women's Emotional Wellness class. She taught us about safe and unsafe boundaries, relationships, choices, the different phases of shame, and much more. One of the most revealing things I learned was that I was unsafe

within myself, and, therefore, attracting unsafe relationships.

Ouch! That was not something I had expected to learn.
However, the old saying, "When the student is ready, the
teacher appears," was so true in my case.

We started out with a class of twelve, and by the time
we graduated, only six remained. Again, this was not an
easy class to take.

You must be willing to do the work within if you want
to benefit on the outside. If you are in a similar place, I
encourage you to seek help from a qualified counselor, and
make a commitment to stick with it so you can be free.

THINK IT OVER...

How might your family react to your decision to start a
business?

How can you involve your spouse in your new business?

In what ways could your children be part of your business?

What entrepreneurial skills could you teach your children?

Who in your life can you rely on for support? List your
potential support network here.

List five ways you will take care of yourself while you
are building your business.

CHAPTER 6
READ THE MANUAL

It's important to learn all you can about network marketing if you truly want to succeed. You must become a lifelong student. Successful network marketers become experts in their fields. They not only know the information, but they constantly think and talk about it. It permeates them and becomes a part of who they are.

If you want to be successful, you need confidence in these four areas: network marketing, your company, your product, and yourself. Much of that confidence comes through knowledge. This isn't knowledge the successful entrepreneurs were born with, and it's not exclusive to them. You can gain the same knowledge and perspective by educating yourself.

If you spend the time to learn more and become a better you, then you can also become an expert and have massive success in your business. There is an old saying: "If you want more than you have—become more than you are!"

When people choose to buy your product or join your business, they are not only buying the company and the product—they are buying YOU! Network marketing is a "people business." It involves connecting with people, finding and meeting their needs, building relationships, and building teams.

As you become a student of sales and relationships, you make yourself a valuable team member and then a leader. Not only will this help you help your team, but it will help you grow your business.

Become a student of personal growth. The better you become, the faster your business will grow.

WHERE DO I BEGIN?

"OK," you say. "I get it. I need to learn all of this stuff. But how? I'm new to this business. I don't even know where to begin!"

The first place to look is within your company. Every company wants its affiliates to be successful, and they usually have a list of resources to help you do just that. Find out what resources your company recommends. Watch all the training videos available on your company website and read through your training materials thoroughly. Ask questions about anything you don't understand or want to learn more about. Your company, your sponsor, and your upline are great resources. Use them!

CORPORATE TRAINING

Find out when the corporate trainings are and participate. You'll learn new and relevant information about your company and your products. Not only that, but many companies highlight their top producers in the trainings; perhaps you'll learn some of their best strategies for building a business. This is an area many people neglect.

You can be one of the first people in your organization to know the latest developments in your company. Attend those trainings!

TEAM LEADER TRAINING

In addition to corporate trainings, teams often have their own meetings. Each team has a leader who typically has been in the business for a few years and achieved a level of success. Very often, he/she will host weekly events for their entire team. These events can be a treasure—a wealth of training and how-to tips for building your new business.

Participate in these trainings whenever possible, and listen to the recordings later if you miss them. Take notes. This is your education, your "classroom," and you will learn from people who didn't just read about network marketing but are out there proving it works.

COMPANY CONVENTION

Most companies also hold annual conventions. Traveling to the convention and booking a hotel room may seem expensive, but it's worth it. Even better, bring your team with you.

Top leaders say that each person who attends a convention adds one hundred new people to their team over time. Why is that? Leverage. For every person you bring who experiences the training and invaluable networking at your convention, you will save many hours of your valuable time training and motivating them yourself.

You also have the opportunity to meet company representatives and top achievers in person. You hear motivational speakers, and you learn how the company is doing. In addition, you learn about new products and the vision for the company. Most importantly, you meet others who are excited about what they're doing and who can share ideas with you.

You learn and are motivated on many levels, and you bring that motivation back with you—and so does your team!

REGIONAL AND LOCAL EVENTS

Regional and local events are the next best thing to keep you and your team inspired and to build momentum. Nothing compares to the energy in a group setting to keep everyone inspired. The more events you and your team attend, the more training and motivation to succeed everyone will come away with—and the faster you will all travel on the road to success and freedom.

MENTORS

Another important source of information is your sponsor—the person who introduced you to your company. If your direct sponsor isn't working his/her business actively, keep going up until you find someone who is. Look for someone who inspires you and who you like. When you choose a mentor, you learn more than just what they do; you learn who they are.

Once you've found a mentor within your company, become an active participant in anything they have to offer. Watch their videos. Read their emails and blogs. Attend the team meetings they lead. Go to the seminars they go to. Ask questions, and always, always, introduce yourself.

The best network marketers are always looking for someone on their teams to train and mentor. As you get to know each other and develop a relationship, they will want to help you!

Success breeds success. Spend time with successful people in your company, and you will learn to think and act like them. In the process, you'll become successful, too.

BOOKS

Outside of your company, there are many great print resources to turn to. Here are some great books to add to your library:

The Business of the 21st Century, Robert Kiyosaki
Beach Money and *Better than Beach Money*, Jordan Adler
How to Win Friends and Influence People, Dale Carnegie
The Four Year Career, Richard Brooke
The Four Year Career for Women, Kimmy Brooke
Think and Grow Rich, Napoleon Hill
The Slight Edge, Jeff Olson
Spirit Driven Success, Dani Johnson
Big Al Tells All series, Tom "Big Al" Schreiter
Excuse Me, Your Life Is Waiting, Lynn Grabhorn
Continuous Sales Improvement, Eric Lofholm
Rock Your Network Marketing Business, Sarah Robbins

Many of these titles are available on audio, so you can listen as you drive or go about your day. The books listed here are just a drop in the bucket. The more you read, the better you will become at network marketing!

COACHING

One of the very best ways to learn more about how to become a successful entrepreneur is to find a professional coach. Even if you have a successful career in the business world, success in network marketing is not guaranteed, as it requires some different skills. Finding a coach who will help you stay on top of your goals and teach you the skills you need in this new arena can make all the difference!

Whether you participate in a virtual event, go to in-person workshops, pay for coaching, subscribe to an email list, or do phone coaching, finding a coach is important. It's a good idea to ask your sponsor for recommendations. In many companies, the team leaders often have guest speakers on their calls. When you feel a connection to a speaker, invest in whatever they have to offer. Remember, you are investing in yourself!

A common quote often heard in our profession is, "You need to work harder on yourself than you do on your business." This saying is true for many reasons, but the most important one is that the better you become as a person, the more successful people you will attract to your team. Educating yourself, while continuing with the daily activities of business-building, will help you achieve massive growth personally and in your business.

KAREN'S PERSONAL DEVELOPMENT SUCCESS STORY

I have always been a high achiever. I wanted to make my parents proud. I got straight As in school, graduating with honors from college with both my BA in English and MA in Rhetoric and Composition. I believed that I could do anything I set my mind to—and I always set the bar high.

When I became a mom, I made a choice to be a mother, gladly giving up my career as a college English professor at Grand Canyon University and my dreams to get my PhD and become an author. Over the years, though, I discovered that, while I loved being a mom, my dreams wouldn't just be shoved under the rug.

When I began building my network marketing business, I began with trepidation. I didn't have any experience, but I had a lot of determination. I immediately began listening to every team and corporate call I could, and I bought every book recommended by my team leaders. I listened to free seminars and paid for coaching. It was during one coaching session that I found my passions again.

Not only did all of that personal development help me build my business, but it also reconnected me to my dreams. Since then, I have earned two promotions with my company, written two books, and even won some awards! I earned my PhD in 2015, and now that my kids are older, I've become a full-time college professor again.

The best part is that, because I've rediscovered who I am, I've found a deeper connection to my husband and my kids. I've learned that I can be present in my home while pursuing my passions. I promise you: Personal development will change your life and give you a confidence in your dreams that you never knew existed.

THINK IT OVER...

How much of a role does personal development play in your life?

What things have you done already that will help you in the area of personal development?

List three ways you can invest in yourself, then create a personal development plan.

CHAPTER 7
FILL YOUR TANK – MAKING CONNECTIONS

If you want to take a trip, you don't start off with an empty tank. In network marketing, your connections are the fuel to fill your tank and keep your business vehicle running. They are your most valuable assets. Our team leader often says, "The size of your database determines the size of your income." Network marketing is all about building relationships with people.

Below are some tips on building your network.

PEOPLE YOU KNOW (YOUR "WARM" MARKET)

It is widely understood that women are naturally the best networkers. We are more collaborative and usually make connections easily. Because of this, we have the edge when it comes to creating and building relationships, which are the heart and soul of network marketing.

It is also a fact that most people know an average of at least 200 to 250 people. These are called your "warm market." We recommend you begin with your warm-market contacts, as they already know you and have rapport with you.

In fact, when you start your new business, one of the first things to do is let your friends, family, and colleagues know about your product. Here is the good part: You already have a comfort level in talking with them, and if you sincerely let them know you would like to practice with them in talking about your product/service, they are more likely to give you grace while you get comfortable. This will help you gain the confidence to meet new people later.

Here are just a few examples of warm-market connections to get you started:

- family members
- friends (Open your cell phone! One of the things people overlook—because it is with them every day—is their cell phone.)
- co-workers
- people you do business with (insurance agents, landscaper, real estate agents, chiropractor, hairdresser, nail tech, pest control tech, veterinarian, home maintenance people, massage therapist, day care provider)
- people you know from church
- people you know from special interest groups (such as PTA)
- business contacts (clients, peers in your industry)
- professional association contacts
- organizations you volunteer time with (United Way, hospitals, food banks, shelters)
- people you know from classes you take (Mommy & Me, cooking, exercise, seminars, workshops, school)
- social media contacts

The best thing to do is to just get started. Make a list of people you know who will love your product and will listen and give you feedback on your presentation. The more you share your products with others, the more comfortable you will be.

PEOPLE YOU DON'T KNOW... YET
(YOUR "COLD" MARKET)

In addition to the 200-plus people you already know, you also meet hundreds—even thousands—of people in your daily life. Do you talk to your grocery store clerk? The other moms at the park? Your waitstaff? Your Uber driver?

Think of each of these people as a new relationship—and potential business partner. Here are some examples:

- people you meet while you are out in everyday life (workplace, grocery or department store, coffee shop, children's school, sporting events)
- referrals from friends/family/co-workers/current customers

We have seen this happen quite often: Someone on our team is looking to meet the CEO of a company or the decision-maker of a key account, and they make the connection because their best friend goes to lunch with that same person every week.

Never underestimate the power of your sphere of influence and who they know. But you must ASK and be as specific as possible. Our brains respond better to recalling information when asked for specific information versus a general question.

One of the ways you can meet people in your community is to join your local Chamber of Commerce and go to their mixers. Local business owners join, and there are often benefits like special "speed networking" events.

Go to their events as a guest first, and find out if the group is a good fit for you. Are the members positive and motivated about growing their businesses? Do they welcome you? Focus on meeting a few new members at each event and developing relationships with them over time. This is the heart of filling your tank.

Another option is to join BNI (Business Networking International), the largest business networking group in the world (bni.com). The format is standardized, regardless of whether you walk into a meeting in England or Arizona. Each person gets sixty seconds in front of the group to talk about his/her business. After these presentations, one or two business owners get ten to fifteen minutes to showcase their business. The goal of the group is for members to exchange referrals to each other's businesses, which makes it an excellent place to make new connections and introduce your business.

In any given city, there are many other networking groups you can join to meet people. You can find them easily with a quick search online. If your product/service is targeted toward a female audience, or you feel more comfortable at a women's-only group, here are a few suggestions to get you started:

National Association of Women Business Owners (NAWBO), www.nawbo.org. There are chapters all over the U.S. This group attracts women business owners with a luncheon format. In some chapters, you can purchase a table for a nominal fee to showcase your product/service before and after the luncheon. There is a featured speaker on various topics, and you will be able to introduce yourself around your lunch table and exchange business cards. This is another ideal way to get the word out about your product and start new relationships.

eWomen Network (ewomennetwork.com) is a group that attracts professional business women and uses the luncheon model. This group has a more organized format with an educational speaker as well as structured networking exercises, which provide a great introduction to other business women. There are chapters in most states, plus

Canada, and members are welcome to visit any chapter.

In recent years, groups like eWomen Network have added online events. Members and guests can share a short "commercial" to promote their business. They include networking exercises, as well.

With the increase in digital meeting technologies, several networking groups have evolved that are totally virtual, requiring no travel outside the home. One example is The Happy Neighborhood Project, which has virtual chapters in many states and cities. Another is Seven, which is similar, but only for women. Both the in-person model and the virtual model have their advantages and disadvantages. We recommend that you experiment with both to find a good fit for you.

KEY POINT

When you are deciding to join any networking group, here are some tips to use in evaluating what will be a good fit for you:

- What is the energy of the group when you first walk in? Are they warm and inviting, or standoffish or competitive?
- What is the cost of membership (joining fee, monthly dues, or the cost of the monthly breakfast/lunch/dinner)?
- Is your product/service a good compliment to the other businesses?

- Are you willing to commit to at least one year of attending the meetings consistently? Remember, trust and rapport are built over time, and people will do business with you when they feel comfortable that you will be there as the contact person. We have seen new people make the mistake of hopping from one group to another, collecting business cards and thinking they will grow their business this way. People value relationships above all else.

Consider having a booth at a trade show or expo.

Find out what local entrepreneurial events are happening in your town. You can call your Chamber of Commerce or use the internet to look up the calendar of events at your local convention center. This is best when you have one to three team members who can go with you to help you represent your company. You can share expenses, support each other, and create teamwork.

There are also virtual expos where attendance is free.

Things to think about:
- What is the cost?
- How many hours/days do you have to display your product/service?
- What target market will this trade show/expo attract?
- Did the event planners do a good job with publicity?
- Is there only one booth allowed per company?
- How many sales will you need to break even and then profit, based on how much the booth costs?

If this is a local church expo, for example, the cost may be low, but most people are with their families and are focused on going to hear the pastor speak; they are not necessarily in a mindset that will be open to hearing about your product/service as they walk by. The key is to put yourself in the mindset of the people walking by your booth and ask yourself if this is an appropriate fit for the cost, time, and effort. It could be a home run or a total disappointment.

On a regional level, if you are a member of a professional association, consider having a booth at their regional or national conference. Again, this is best done with one to three team members.

If you are already plugged into a network of any kind, create ways to meet and get to know more people in that network. For example, you might invite people one at a time to meet you for coffee or lunch, allowing you to build a relationship and eventually do business together. These one-on-one meetings are vital in creating meaningful connections.

More and more people are using the internet to build their businesses. Utilizing social media sites, such as Facebook, Instagram, TikTok, LinkedIn, and Twitter, can allow you to meet people you wouldn't meet in person. New social media sites are popping up every day. Find one that fits your personality.

What is your niche market? You already have a built-in network of people to talk to, based on your life experience. Think about your current career, evaluate your strengths, and go play in your sandbox.

What does that mean? For example, you may be a dental hygienist. You already know the terminology used in your industry, which will help you establish trust and rapport with other hygienists. Now you just add to the conversation snippets about your product and service.

Maybe your niche market is talking to high-income women business owners. Focus on that market and become the expert known in that niche.

What are your hobbies? Your hobbies will automatically draw you to others who share the same passion, which again helps you establish trust and rapport. Hobbies are an excellent way to meet others and strike up a natural conversation.

Bottom line: The more "strangers" you can turn into friends, the more success you will have in life and in your business. The suggestions in this chapter of ways to meet people will most likely challenge you to get out of your comfort zone by connecting with people you don't know. This may cause you some anxiety at first, so remember your why, step through your fear, and just try it!

One of the things Kristi does before walking into a networking event is to take a couple of minutes to ask God for divine connections regarding who she is supposed to meet that day. That alleviates any pressure about needing to go around the room and gather everyone's business card, and it frees her to relax and enjoy quality conversations and make new friends.

Be creative in turning a cold contact into a warm contact by developing a relationship with them—whether in person, online, or on the phone. People do business with those they know, like, and trust! You will be amazed at the lifelong friendships you will create and the satisfaction you will feel in knowing you made a difference in people's lives with your product and your business opportunity.

With the many uncertainties in the world, now more than ever people are looking and praying for a solution. You could be it! Don't ever pre-judge; just consistently develop relationships and present your opportunity to others. You will be amazed at the results!

THINK IT OVER...

Take five minutes and make a list of the people you know. Remember to simply write down everyone you think of without pre-judgment and without stopping. When five minutes have passed, circle the ten people you think are most likely to love your product and who you feel most comfortable with. Remember, successful network marketers constantly update, revise, and add new names to their list. Schedule time once a month to do this exercise.

CHAPTER 8
STEP ON THE GAS

Now that you have met people by using some of the ideas in the previous chapter, it is time to pull out of the driveway and onto the road to your success! The following ideas and techniques will shave months off your learning curve and help increase your earning curve.

Before we begin, we would like to clarify the information we are about to share with you in this chapter. In network marketing, you will hear quite often, "We SHARE our product or service; we don't SELL." Yet the truth is, every time we ask someone to consider pulling out their credit card for our products, we are involved in a sales experience.

Many people have a negative impression about selling because they have had a bad experience (like having their driver's license held hostage at a car dealership so a salesperson can pressure them to sign a contract). When asked, most people would say people in sales are pushy and not to be trusted. If this is your personal belief, then we are here to suggest it is possible to share the product or service you love and believe in AND also learn some sales skills that will help you be successful, while you remain true to yourself and keep your friends!

Sales = service. When you approach each appointment thinking, "How can I best serve this person (in their personal life or business)?" it shifts your paradigm and how you build your business. People will sense that you are being authentic and be attracted to your energy.

Let's get started!

WHAT DO I SAY?

One of the most effective ways you can start a conversation is to take the pressure and focus off yourself and get to know the other person using the F.O.R.M. technique. It stands for Family, Occupation, Recreation, and Motivation or Money.

Your goal is to find out about the other person using these ideas as starting points. This is not an "interrogation" where you pepper questions at a stranger. Use a couple of ideas from each section, and show genuine interest by listening to the responses and getting to know the person. The conversation should flow easily from one topic to the next.

Key Point

Do not make the mistake of trying to talk all about yourself or give a full-blown presentation to someone about your company, opportunity,

product, or service. When you meet someone, be there to meet them and exchange contact information. Set up a separate time to get together and learn about each other's businesses.

Here are some opening questions in each of the four categories to help you get started:

FAMILY & FRIENDS

- Did you grow up here in (insert your state)?
- Are you married?
- Do you have any kids?
- Do you have any pets? What kind?
- Did you like growing up in the city/country? Do your parents still live there?
- Do you keep in touch with any childhood/college friends?

OCCUPATION

- What kind of work do you do?
- What do you like about your job?
- What's the most challenging thing about your job?
- Do you like your boss/coworkers?
- Is this your dream job and if not, what is?
- Why did you choose this profession, or how did you fall into this career?
- What's the worst job you've ever had? What made it the worst?

RECREATION

- What do you like to do for fun?
- What would you do if you had the whole day to yourself?
- How do you like to unwind after a long day?
- What's your favorite type of food?
- Do you like to play any sports?
- What kind of music do you like?
- Do you like to travel?
- What is your favorite place?

MOTIVATION/MONEY

- What are you passionate about? How did you get into that?
- When you were a child, what did you want to be when you grew up?
- If you didn't have to work, what would you do with your time?
- Are you open to having residual income to help pay for (your home, car, vacation)?

Meeting with a new prospect can be exciting because of his or her life experiences, business background, children, and travels. One of the richest rewards in our industry is the people we meet and the lifelong friends we make. In the very near future, you will look back and be surprised at how making the choice of owning your own business has added so many positive aspects to your journey. Have FUN!

When Kristi's daughter was eight, she taught her the F.O.R.M. technique over breakfast, because Jade tended to be a little shy in social situations. In the car on the way to school, Jade shared that one of her friends incessantly talked about her family's ancestry, so Kristi suggested she use F.O.R.M. questions to find out other facts about her friend. Problem solved! Now, as a college student, Jade uses this framework to create relationships in her college organizations.

This technique can be used in everyday situations with any person you are creating a relationship with, so don't limit yourself to using it just for business contacts.

THE SALES MOUNTAIN

One of the master sales trainers in the world is our personal mentor of several years, Eric Lofholm (saleschampion.com). He was mentored by and eventually became business partners with Donald Moine, PhD, who is one of the experts in the field of sales and marketing psychology. Eric was also a top producer for acclaimed national speaker Tony Robbins. When Lofholm started his own sales coaching business, Robbins hired him back to train his sales staff.

Lofholm created the Sales Mountain, which is a culmination of decades of perfecting a systematic, step-by-step approach to sales. If it's done in a logical order as intended, this system will help you have more success building your business.

We have used this training with our teams, and people who never had any sales background start having better results. Why? Because once you understand that you don't have to be naturally gifted with sales skills, and that selling can be learned and duplicated by you and your team, you can take the pressure off yourself. Remember, you are just sharing a product or service that you love. But there is a process to doing it that, when followed, will bring you better results. This is the Sales Mountain.

Lofholm teaches us first to understand that selling equals service. Selling is about leading—moving people to action. Selling, influence, and persuasion are learned skills. Your prospect is silently begging to be led because you have a product/service that they need, and you are the one perceived as the expert.

The Sales Mountain

6. CLOSE ⟷ 7. OBJECTIONS

SWEET SPOT
Top 25%

5. SHARING BENEFITS   8. FOLLOW UP

4. ASSESSING NEEDS

3. TRUST & RAPPORT   9. REFERRALS

2. APPOINTMENT SETTING

1. LEAD GENERATION

Add value to your customer and always approach people with honor and integrity. The diagram shown on the

previous page illustrates Lofholm's Sales Mountain. If you imagine approaching a new prospect starting on the bottom left side of the mountain, and you follow each of these steps in order, without skipping any, you will be able to achieve more success. This technique actually mimics the natural progression of how a relationship is established. If you try to skip a step, your prospect will feel uncomfortable and will keep up his or her psychological guard against you. It will be much harder to ask for the order and be successful in closing the sale.

1. LEAD GENERATION

The purpose of generating a lead is simply to gather more contacts. This is where using the F.O.R.M. questions helps you get to know your prospect. Make sure you immediately add each person to your database.

2. APPOINTMENT SETTING

The next step in the process is simply to make the appointment to share your product or business opportunity. Once the appointment is made, politely end the conversation. Although you may be excited to share your product or service right then, this is not the time to deliver your presentation. Many new people make this mistake, and then your prospect thinks he or she has enough information to make a decision, when, in reality, they don't.

3. BUILDING TRUST AND RAPPORT

This step is critical, especially if you are connecting with someone who is new to you. Find common ground and develop a rapport with your prospect. Do not skip this step! Imagine going on a first date with someone and, five minutes into dinner, your date declares, "I am in love with you. Will you marry me?" Most people would react by thinking, "Stalker! I need to change my phone number!"

If, however, the appropriate amount of time passes for the couple to get to know each other, develop rapport, and mutually fall in love, asking the same question would have a much different reaction. It is the same in the sales process. People want to know you care about them before you tell them all about you, your product, and your opportunity. People want to know how much you care before they care how much you know.

If you traveled to a foreign country and took the time to learn a few key words or phrases to get around, it would be easier and more enjoyable to connect with people. One tip for establishing this communication with your prospects is to realize that everyone has one of four different communication styles (Tom "Big Al" Schreiter has free resources available to learn more at bigalbooks.com). Read the four color descriptions below and identify your personal style. Then practice using this knowledge with everyone you meet. You will, within minutes, be able to talk to your prospects in their language. Using these key phrases will help you connect with your prospects and create positive results faster.

YELLOW COMMUNICATION STYLE:

HOW TO IDENTIFY A YELLOW:

They are friendly and kind. They will put others' needs before their own. They will start talking about you before they talk about themselves. They are not motivated by money.

- Clothes: They may wear cottons or comfortable clothes, sensible shoes, little/no makeup; they are not flashy.

- Occupations: professional helper, fundraiser, volunteer, massage therapist, health care worker, ministry professional, psychologist, school teacher

What turns them off: talking about compensation plans, the business opportunity, direct eye contact. Don't start a meeting with them by jumping right into your presentation. Build rapport first.

Negative side: They are often indecisive, base their opinions on what others think, and don't enjoy being at the front of the room doing presentations.

Key words to their language: help, love, security, friends, family

BLUE COMMUNICATION STYLE:

HOW TO IDENTIFY A BLUE:

Blues are outgoing and people-oriented. They enjoy being the center of attention. They are visionary/big picture people, which makes them great motivators, prospectors, and promoters.

- Clothes: They tend to wear colorful, hip/trendy clothing. Make-up/hair/nails are important to them, and great shoes are must!
- Occupations: salespeople, travel agents, tour guides, entrepreneurs

What turns them off: too much detail, too many tasks at once

Negative side: They are usually late. They are non-stop talkers (during movies, presentations, etc.) and can be easily distracted. They tend to struggle with follow up, and it's hard for them to stay focused.

Key words to their language: people, fun, party, vacations

RED COMMUNICATION STYLE:

HOW TO IDENTIFY A RED:

Reds like to be in charge and are often great organizers. They like to be at the front of the room doing presentations. They need to be recognized, and they can enjoy competitions. They will use brief answers when talking with you.

- Clothes: They tend to wear quality suits/dresses and shoes. They like to present a successful image.
- Occupations: CEO's, managers, salespeople, business owners

What turns them off: people who don't make eye contact, talk too much, and don't have confidence when approaching them.

Negative side: Reds tend to be headstrong, judgmental, and competitive. They often think they know everything, and they might interrupt you while you're talking. They usually make up their minds in the first one to three minutes of your presentation.

Key words to their language: money, recognition, power, win. Keep your sentences brief. With this person, building rapport is less important than getting to the point of your conversation.

GREEN COMMUNICATION STYLE:

HOW TO IDENTIFY A GREEN:

Greens are technical, analytical, detail-oriented, linear thinkers. They are great organizers.

- Clothes: They tend to be conservatively dressed, without flashy colors.
- Occupations: technical fields, IT, quality control, bookkeeping, tax accounting

What turns them off: being kept waiting, making up answers, and being unprepared.

Negative side: They will want to heavily read and research everything to make sure they are making the "right" decision. Because of this, they very rarely make a decision on the spot.

Key words to their language: data, facts, research, information. Facts are a great way to build credibility with a green.

4. ASSESSING NEEDS

Once you have determined your prospect's communication style, it's very important to ask them questions to find out what they are doing to grow their business, achieve better health, create more income, etc. Listen and assess if your product or service can help this person.

Remember, your goal is to help others. You may find out they are satisfied with the way things are in the personal, financial, spiritual, or business aspects of their life. If that is the case, then you can go right to step nine and ask for referrals. If not, proceed to Step Five.

5. SHARING BENEFITS

Describe how your product or service can help generate more business for your prospect, help them create better health, save them time and money, etc. Be prepared to share a story of how someone similar to them received benefits from using your products or from joining your company as an affiliate. Share with the person how you can help her. Focus on her needs, not yours.

6. ACTUALLY ASKING

Once you have followed Steps 1-5, you are now at the peak of the Sales Mountain, or the "sweet spot." Ask if they are ready to move forward, and then be silent. Most people avoid this step. They do not directly ask for the sale, or, if they do, they do not remain silent for the prospect to answer.

You will notice there is an arrow going back and forth between Step Six and Step Seven. This is where you "elegantly dance" with your prospect. If they give you an objection, ask a specific question to understand the reason for the objection (see Step 7). Then solve the problem, ask for the order again, and remain silent. Once you are in this sweet spot with the prospect, you are at the point where it is easier to lead them to making a decision.

7. OBJECTION HANDLING

Most people, especially women, have trouble with this step because they are afraid of being rejected or because they don't know how to respond to an objection effectively. If you approach this step like you're a detective trying to uncover how you can help solve your prospect's needs, then it isn't as scary.

Know that usually the first objection isn't the true reason they are saying no. The prospect is trying to buy some time before they decide. An objection is just a question that your prospect has that you didn't cover during your presentation.

Here is the great news: In the network marketing industry, no matter what product or service you represent, there are only a handful of objections you will hear. Some of them are:

- I don't have the money.
- I don't have the time.
- I need to check with my spouse/significant other.
- I need to think about it.
- I need more information.
- I already tried something similar and it didn't work.

- I'm not interested.

TECHNIQUES FOR YOUR TOOL KIT

Here are several different techniques to address these objections.

STORY
One of the most powerful ways to handle an objection is with a story. Stories are so persuasive because they act as invisible selling. Stories also suspend time. Identify true stories that address the prospect's situation. One way to start the story is by saying, "That reminds me of a story of someone who was in a similar situation. Let me share with you what they did…"

QUESTION
You can answer an objection with a question. For example:

Objection: "The price is too high."
Response: "By too high, what exactly do you mean?"
Response: "How much is too much?"
Response: "Compared to what?"

Objection: "I don't have the time." Response: "When will you have the time?"
Response: "On a scale of one to ten, how motivated are you to move forward?"
Response: "What do you mean by that?"

ISOLATE

Isolating an objection is a favorite technique, because it is very effective and easy to learn.

Objection: "I don't have the money."
Response: "I can appreciate that. Other than the money, is there anything else that is preventing you from taking action today?" Be silent and listen for their answer.

Objection: "I don't have the time."
Response: "Other than the time, is there anything else preventing you from moving forward today?" Be silent.

INVESTIGATE

"Tell me more about that." Listen to what your prospect is saying and assess if you can help solve the problem.

Always be sensitive to your prospect's needs. There may be personal situations going on in their life that have nothing to do with whether or not they will use your product. Remember, a no today doesn't necessarily mean NO forever. Do not take a rejection/objection personally. It's all about timing.

Objection: "I love your system, but I can't afford it right now."
Response: "I understand. Other than the money, is there anything else keeping you from moving forward today?" Be quiet and let them answer.
Response: "When would it be okay for me to follow up with you?" Once the prospect gives you a date, make SURE to put it in your calendar and CALL HER BACK!
The key here, regardless of the objection, is simply to ask questions. If your prospect says no, it does not mean forever; it just means that, for that moment in time, it isn't right for them.

8. FOLLOW UP

If your prospect chooses not to get started, they fall below the sweet spot. Now you are headed down the right side of the Sales Mountain. Once this happens, it is harder to re-create the same excitement the person had when you first did the presentation. The key here is to be consistent with your follow-up. Get your prospect's permission to contact them. (i.e., "Would it be okay if I followed up with you?") Agree on a date and time, write it down, and make sure you follow through.

KEY POINT

Most customers will not move to action until you have contacted them five to seven times, no matter what methods of communication you use. However, most people give up after the first or second follow up, and their prospects will most likely sign up later with someone else who does follow up multiple times!

9. REFERRALS

Always ask for referrals, and find ways to refer business to your prospect to help build their business if they have one. Be specific in the type of referral you are looking for: "Who do you know who is a chiropractor/insurance agent/real estate agent?" It is easier for people to recall someone's name quickly from their memory when you give a specific request than if you say, "I am looking for people who want to be healthy."

Understand the Sales Mountain and practice it until it becomes an automatic part of your process for meeting with prospects. In addition, the following ideas will help you hone your skills and build your team.

DEVELOP YOUR THIRTY-SECOND COMMERCIAL

Create a concise, easy-to-understand thirty-second commercial or "interest-creating remark" to have ready at a moment's notice. When someone asks, "What do you do?" you will be able to tell the person in thirty seconds about your product or service, with the end result being that they will want to reconnect with you to find out more.

An example of how you can share what you do is using a simple script for your commercial. "I help people in (the prospect's industry) with (state the benefit of your product/service)." This is easy to remember, and it immediately creates curiosity with your prospect because you appeal to the question in their mind, "What's in it for me?" This script is also simple enough to teach your team how to effectively duplicate what you did.

APPOINTMENT SETTING

Some people will have no problem setting appointments; others may find this part a challenge because they fear rejection. When you ask someone for an appointment, do not make the mistake of trying to give your entire presentation to them right then and there. Set the appointment, and then be courteous and end the phone call.

If you are talking in person, end the conversation about your business and switch the topic to something else.

You can spot a novice in a room full of people because they are the ones who thrust a business card at someone, then a brochure, and then invite their prospect to a presentation. By this time, the prospect has the "Where's the exit?" look on their face and will try to get away from the person as fast as possible. The novice will then wonder why people will not return calls—ever.

Be professional, courteous, and respectful. These attributes go a long way with people remembering you in a positive way.

An example of a simple phone script to use may be, "Hi, this is (your name) from (your company). We met at (event). Did I catch you at a good time?" It is good business practice to ask that question, because if the person is running out the door or has a sick child, it's best to ask when a better day/time to call back would be. If you get a positive response, then you can say, "You had expressed interest in wanting to know more about our (product/service). Are you available either Tuesday or Thursday, at (time)?" Agree on the day/time, and then, as stated above, end the phone call courteously.

Make sure to write down the appointment and follow up.

THE BUSINESS PRESENTATION

When you first start sharing your product, service, or business opportunity with people, it's a good idea to involve the person who got you started and has more experience.

Be sure to introduce your prospect to your sponsor and your sponsor to your prospect in such a way that you compliment both people to each other. Highlight each person's skills, accomplishments, and qualities. This helps bring credibility to your company, to yourself, and to your prospect. Then step back and let your sponsor walk through the first few presentations.

Once you feel comfortable, ask your sponsor to be there for support as you gradually take over the driver's seat. This is key for your success, because you will be able to take notes on the questions being asked and how they are answered.

This also indirectly trains your prospect, should they

decide to join your team, because they get to see the process in action.

You will make mistakes. You will not know all the answers. If you ever learned to drive a stick shift car, do you remember what that was like? Grinding gears, popping the clutch, the terror of having to stop on a hill and trying not to roll backwards when the light turned green while drivers behind you grew impatient or tried to back up so they wouldn't get hit… Little by little, it got easier. And, today, you can do it without thinking.

This is the learning process for anything new. Recognize your fear as just part of the process, put in the key, step on the gas, and get started anyway!

FOLLOW UP, FOLLOW UP, FOLLOW UP

One of the keys to build a successful business is having a follow-up system that you utilize consistently. Many, many sales are left on the table because the person fails to communicate after the first meeting or after the presentation. Often, a person might stop calling after the first unanswered call because she thinks it is a personal rejection. The more likely story is that people are leading busy lives and fail to return calls. Remember, it takes five to seven contacts before your prospect will move to action with you and get started.

TRACKING

To help you keep track of your follow-ups, create a tracking system you are comfortable using. The tracking system could be online or off-line, using technology or something as simple as pen and paper. There is no right or wrong way, as long as you are consistent and you know, at a glance, where you are with any given prospect.

Some suggestions for your tracking sheet:
- name
- phone number
- where you met
- appointment set
- presentation done
- follow-up call
- date signed up as a customer or affiliate
- training done (if applicable to your product or service)

KEY POINT

Just because you hear no today, does not mean it is a no forever. If the prospect agrees to you following up, put the future date in your tracking system and then be courteously persistent.

For many people, timing is crucial when they are ready to use your product/service. Remember, this is part of keeping your tank full.

In Kristi's case, when she was first introduced to her current company, she said, "I would never use your product." Two short months later, circumstances changed. She reconnected with the person, and she now has a huge team that is growing every month.

KAREN'S STORY

After moving to Texas in 2010, I took out all of my old contacts—two years' worth of business cards and contact forms! I went through each contact one by one, calling them just to let them know I had moved and to see if they were still interested in my product. There were people I had followed up with consistently over the years, but had not heard from for a long time. As I was leaving my phone number for one woman I had met a year earlier, I got cut off, so I called back to leave my number. This time she answered! When I told her who I was, she got so excited!

"Someone just showed me this, but I could never go with anyone else after all the follow-up you have done! I'm ready to get started. Let's make an appointment for next week."

Not only did I gain a new customer, but I inspired someone to do better at her own follow-up! The moral of the story? You never know! Just keep following up until the person tells you to stop.

USE YOUR COMPANY'S TOOLS.

Every company has marketing tools that have been carefully researched to be the most effective at selling your product or service and introducing your company's business opportunity. Use them!

Your product or service can be one of the best tools you have, so make sure you are a product of your product! If you are in a health and wellness company, make sure you use the product so you can have your own personal story to share. If you are in a beauty products company, then your face is your biggest asset in selling your products.

You must be authentic and have integrity. People can sense it immediately if you do not. They may never say it out loud; they just will not return your calls and will align with someone else with whom they resonate better.

TRAIN YOUR NEW TEAM MEMBERS.

Your company has an established system and checklist of how to properly train your new team members. First of all, make sure you follow the system, become comfortable with it, and then teach it to your team. Educate them about the basics of network marketing with books such as Jordan Adler's Beach Money or Richard Brooke's The Four Year Career. It's important to remember that it takes a three-to-five-year commitment before your new business partner will see significant paychecks.

You never know who will be your next business builder who will go on to lead a huge team—so your job is to just get each person started. Do not build their team for them; teach them how to do it themselves. Otherwise, you will have a weak team that will eventually diminish.

Keep in mind also that training is an ongoing process for everyone who chooses to be successful in network marketing. After you do the initial training with your new team member, it is her responsibility to take it from there. Make yourself available for questions and ongoing support, and point them to the ongoing training resources. But your basic training job with them is done at that point.

THINK IT OVER...

Take a moment to examine your old ideas about selling. If you have negative feelings about selling, shift your mindset to "How can I serve this person, and what are the benefits of my product or service for them?"

Did you know that sales is a learned skill? Write down an accountability partner who you can practice the Sales Mountain process with—someone who can give you gentle feedback.

In looking at the four color personality styles, which one do you relate to most? How can you utilize this knowledge to communicate better with your family, friends, and people you meet?

Who can you practice F.O.R.M. with?

Brainstorm some ideas for your thirty-second commercial. Think "value/benefit," and keep it concise. Practice it out loud until you can say it without hesitation.

CHAPTER 9
LEAD A CARAVAN

One of the greatest aspects of network marketing is the network! As you bring new people into your business, you build a team of networkers who will help you grow your business, even as they grow their own businesses. As you progress in your business and become a team leader, there are some important things to remember that will help you grow your team and lead them to their dreams while you are reaching yours.

DUPLICATION IS VITAL TO YOUR SUCCESS.

One of the best features of the network marketing business model is that you do NOT have to be a great salesperson to be successful! This is not about you getting thousands of customers to use your product/service.

The successful network marketer only needs to find a few people who want to use the product and a few who also want to build a business—and teach them exactly what to do.

Once you get a few others started in the business, it's not just about you anymore. You never stop sponsoring new people, but your focus needs to be on team-building and helping others duplicate your success. Learning how to teach others to duplicate what has worked for you is the key to massive growth and success in our type of business.

Here are some tips that can make all the difference:
- Have a system for getting someone started.
- Keep it simple.
- Teach it consistently.

Many people who start a network marketing team make the mistake of not teaching an easily duplicatable system. Or they jump from idea to idea regarding how to train their team. Then, in the eternal quest to find the "perfect" system or a shortcut, the team will become confused and growth will slow down as the team members get bogged down in learning the details of each new way.

Invariably, you will be excited about starting your own business; resist the urge to come up with new and creative ideas about how to get started. You will lose precious time and momentum trying to reinvent your company's system instead of using tried-and-true methods from the top income earners. Once you have mastered your company's process, then you can tailor it slightly for your personality.

One of the most successful and respected people in network marketing today, Jordan Adler, wisely states, "If an eight-year-old cannot follow what you are doing, then it's too difficult...Simple is key!" The bottom line is to know your product/service and learn the easiest way to teach others. Then do not deviate from that message, no matter what others around you are doing.

LEADERSHIP

Once you have a few other people sharing your product and your message, you have a team. You have moved into a position of leadership, since they are looking to you for guidance. Always keep in mind that your team will do what you do, so pay attention to your own thoughts, words, and actions!

There are several ways you can be a leader. You may be comfortable standing at the front of the room conducting monthly trainings. But if you are not, that's okay. There are very powerful leaders who grow their teams one by one, sitting across the table from people in their homes. There are still others who have little personal contact with their team members, but lead by means of zoom calls, e-mails, Facebook posts, and videos.

The how is individual, but the what includes these ten leadership principles:

- Be a self-starter. Don't wait to always be told what to do.
- Lead by example. Do yourself what you want your team to do. They watch your actions more than your words.
- Encourage each new distributor to believe in
- themselves.
- Provide inspiration and vision for your team.

- Teach the skills and system that your reps need to succeed.
- Stay positive always.
- Take responsibility. Don't blame or be a victim.
- Don't let challenges stop you. Learn to be resilient.
- Recognize the efforts and promotions of team members.
- Respect others always and have an attitude of gratitude.

The important thing is to be aware of your own mindset and energy and to be courageous enough to work on yourself and make changes if necessary. Stepping into your greatness as a leader is more internal than external. The more you develop your own skills and mindset, the more you will have to share with your team. Always be in the process of personal growth and becoming better. True leaders never feel that they know it all; they are perpetual students of growth.

TEAM-BUILDING

When you first start building your business, it will often feel like you are working hard and building your team single- handedly. Our best advice is to set a goal for your first year of personally signing up (sponsoring) twenty-four to thirty business builders, approximately two to three per month. Statistically, one person in that group of twenty-four will take off and build a huge team under you. But at the outset, you won't know which one is going to be that superstar. So make it a goal to just sign up your twenty-four to thirty.

Remember not to pre-judge. There is an old saying in our industry: "The people you think will be a superstar won't, and the people you think won't will!"

Once you have twenty-four to thirty people signed up on your team, the focus becomes teaching them to duplicate what you've done.

Think of your business as a tree developing a strong root system that grows automatically over time. A tree with strong roots won't blow over in a storm. It results in a healthy tree that will thrive for years to come.

GETTING TO 100

Once you get your first twenty-four to thirty distributors on your team, your next goal is to grow that number to 100 as quickly as possible. The reason is this: It can often seem like it takes forever to build that first group of 100. But, as more people from this group of 100 sponsor their own new affiliates, you are likely to see faster team growth. Every subsequent group of 100 new distributors typically happens quicker than the last.

BECOME A LEADER OF LEADERS

Once the top achievers on your team start to emerge, it is time to help them become leaders of their own teams. This is how you duplicate yourself so you can move on to find new business builders without having to personally manage everyone on your growing team. If you do not do this, you will burn out! If you do develop leaders, your team can grow to unlimited heights, and you will still have the energy to enjoy the process.

Learn to be aware of your up-and-coming leaders' personal behavioral styles and strengths, and then help them refine and expand their skills. It will always be about people skills and the relationships they build first and the product second, which goes back to the importance of on-going training and personal growth.

Teach your new leaders to honor others and to respect the differences in personalities, customs, beliefs, and individual styles. Encourage your leaders to read books by the classic personal growth authors like Earl Nightingale, Dale Carnegie, Jim Rohn, and Zig Ziglar.

Having leadership retreats once or twice a year encourages future growth and replenishment of the body, mind, and spirit. Your company may provide them; if not, create your own.

Express encouragement and gratitude to your team regularly, which will help them keep going on their own journeys to success. Look for opportunities to recognize achievements, company promotions, and general excellence in your team members at all times. (Remember, some people work harder for recognition than for money!)

And always be ready to help your teammates who ask for help. You could be the difference between them sticking with the journey long enough to be successful and achieve their dreams or dropping out too soon and failing. As Zig Ziglar says, "Help enough people get what they want, and you will get what you want."

THINK IT OVER...

Who has been a significant leader for you in your life?
What characteristics do they have?
What leadership traits do you already have that can serve you in your new business?

CHAPTER 10
GET PAST DETOURS AND BUMPS IN THE ROAD:
DEALING WITH CHALLENGES

Question: What is the #1 reason people fail in a network marketing business?
Answer: Because they quit too soon!

If you were on an important road trip from San Diego to New York, why would you quit and give up your journey when you only got as far as Omaha, Des Moines, or Pittsburgh? Why would someone stop and quit their business before reaching their goals and dreams? Because they fall prey to one or more detours on their journey. Be aware of these bumps in the road so they don't catch you off guard:

1. The bump in the road called Disappointment, when someone says no to buying your product/service or joining your team as a distributor when you are certain they would benefit from it or be an awesome team builder.
2. The barrier called Discouragement, when one of your new team members never even gets started (also known as the perpetual "getting ready to get ready" syndrome).

3. The pothole called Deception, when someone on your team promises to build a huge organization under you and then does nothing, or leaves your group for another company.

4. The detour called Dismay, when some of your team members drop out halfway through their own journey to financial freedom.

The reality is that many affiliates will stop building their business in their first few months or years. Momentum doesn't happen overnight, and new team members without a strong why and a solid inner foundation may not make it. Every successful network marketer has had to deal with this reality. You can either use the high dropout factor as an excuse to quit yourself, or keep going on your own journey. The choice is totally yours.

As caring and compassionate women, we may also fall into the trap of trying to carry inactive team members on our backs in a misguided effort to help them as we journey down the road to freedom. This will only slow down your own business growth. Typically, your efforts to carry others who are not working the business will not motivate them; it just makes them dependent on you. We strongly caution you not to confuse caring with carrying! To quote the great female network marketing pioneer Kim Klaver, "You can't drag others across the finish line."

PERSONAL COPING STRATEGIES

Here's how to cope with the detours and bumps in the road, so you don't let the actions of others drag you down and put the enemy of doubt in your mind.

THE BIG PICTURE

To complete your journey and be successful, you must stay focused on the big picture—your why—and think long term when negative situations arise. Disappointments are only temporary. Remember the deep emotional why, the dream that drove you to start your business. Revisit your vision board and refocus on your goals. Get support from your sponsor or other trusted leaders in your company. Stay focused on your big picture goals and dreams, and they will lead you like a shining beacon on the path to your greatness and your freedom.

THINK LONG TERM

Typically, thinking long term in network marketing means only five to seven years! Could you keep going for five to seven years if you KNEW you would reach your destination and your dreams would come true in that timeframe?

There is an old saying in network marketing that is as true today as it will be years from now. "It's easy to pay the price when the promise is clear."

KEY POINT

Once you have found the right product and company for you, MAKE A COMMITMENT to

yourself and your family that you will work your business *for three to five years, part time or full time, NO MATTER WHAT.*

Then **take action every day** to move your business forward. It doesn't need to be a lot of hours per day. Remember, most people build their fortune part time around their jobs, family, and other life commitments.

But your effort does need to be FOCUSED AND CONSISTENT. Starting and stopping will severely slow down your business growth, or even kill it. Consistency of action is the key, and big picture thinking will keep you on the path and in the game until you reach your destination—FREEDOM!

STRATEGIES TO MINIMIZE TEAM ATTRITION

The truth is, it will probably take a few years of consistent effort for a network marketer's residual income to replace his/her job income, and a few more years after that for most to finance their goals and dreams.

Many people in today's world simply do not have the discipline to consistently put in five to seven years of prospecting, sharing their product/service, sponsoring, and training. And sometimes life happens and things get in the way. Therefore, attrition on your team is to be expected. It is part of the building process.

Here are four strategies to help minimize your team's attrition rate and keep them in the game until they have enough success to never want to quit:
- Work closely with new team members you sponsor in their first thirty days, and help them have success

right out of the gate. There is nothing like getting a check right away to keep a new person excited.

- Build community on your team by getting together consistently, online or offline. Make your team members feel a sense of belonging to something bigger than themselves, and make it fun. Building relationships can do wonders for team longevity!

- Keep in touch regularly with your team, especially as your team grows outside of your geographic area. Building long-distance relationships is a critical skill if you want to create and maintain a big team.

- Most importantly, get your team to attend events as much as possible. This includes both live and online company events, and especially the annual convention. The positive group energy at these gatherings will keep your team members enthusiastic and motivated to go home and work their business in a way that nothing else can. Become a promoter of these trainings and events, with the goal of keeping your team in the game until they have enough success to never want to quit.

AN IMPORTANT SECRET

Despite the above strategies, you will have team members who quit your business. Here's a secret many people new to network marketing don't know: The majority of your income will be generated from only a few key people on your team. These are your aces, the one in twenty-four to thirty people previously mentioned who will build a huge team under you and create those key legs that will take your business toward your dreams. So don't spend sleepless nights over those that drop out. They were not your aces.

How do you know when you have an ace on your team?

1. They take responsibility for learning how to do the business without waiting for you to do it for them.

2. They take consistent action without needing to be pushed.

3. They don't complain or quit over their own challenges.

4. They show up for events and training calls.

5. They build their own large group of affiliates and become leaders without you holding their hand along the way.

Find five to ten of these aces, and focus on encouraging them as leaders. Learn to let go of the rest, because many of them will not make it to the finish line.

UNREALISTIC EXPECTATIONS

Question: What is another big reason people fail in network marketing?

Answer: Unrealistic expectations.

Our society has taught us to expect instant results—the "just add water and stir" mentality. Because of this, and because some network marketers have spread hype about what can be earned upfront in our profession, it is not uncommon to see new reps quit when they don't see huge checks in their first ninety days in business.

Here's another place to pause and take a long-term view.

If you had invested thousands of dollars in law school, how long would you expect to work before just breaking even? If you borrowed thousands of dollars to start a traditional business or franchise, would you expect to be in the profit zone immediately after opening? It would take years of hard work just to be in the black.

In the network marketing business model, the good news is that you can recoup your investment in a short period of time, as opposed to years. The bad news is that you will not typically see big dollars at first, relative to the time and effort you put into your new venture. Be sure you understand this. You're exchanging a lot of work and little return in the beginning for less work and a bigger return later.

KEY POINT

Do NOT look at your checks during your first six months and ask yourself, "Is it worth it?" Our business takes time. Again, keep your eyes on your why and your goals. And remember big picture thinking!

Revisit this question after your network marketing business is one to two years old. By then, the power of duplication and leveraging yourself should have kicked in, and you will know the answer to that question. If you have taken consistent action, you should have a growing business with a steady income, and you won't need to ask yourself that question again. After a few years, you should see major progress toward your goals and dreams as your bank account grows.

IS IT WORTH IT?

Where else can you invest a few hundred dollars, work part time for several years, and have the potential to be financially free, with income coming to you automatically each month? Ask any network marketer who has survived the disappointments, detours, and bumps in the road to reach their dreams—it is so worth it!

They reached their destination by working consistently, thinking long term, having faith and patience, getting support from their team and their families, having fun, sharing a product or service they love, and helping others to achieve their dreams. Network marketing can be the most rewarding journey you will ever take, as long as you keep your perspective, keep your eyes on your future goals, and decide to enjoy the journey!

NETWORK MARKETING AND THE SNOWBALL

What if you got paid to push a big snowball over a mountain? Have you ever tried to push a snowball uphill? At first, it feels like you are the only one pushing. After a while, a couple of people join you and start helping you push. It's still hard, but not as lonely.

A bit later, there are a few more people pushing the snowball, and, even though it is growing, the load feels lighter because you are now part of a team. You are all working together for a common purpose.

After more time elapses, you see that you are closer to the top of the mountain. You look around and realize that your team has doubled and tripled since you last counted, as each person found more people to join the group effort.

At last, you reach the top and find that you don't have to push the snowball uphill anymore. In fact, it is poised to roll down the other side of the mountain. You get ready for that. The snowball starts down and gathers a little momentum, then a lot of momentum. As it rolls downhill faster and faster, it's all you can do to hang on for the ride of your life.

THAT is the journey of network marketing!

THINK IT OVER...

Would you quit if someone says no to your product or business? How about five people? What about ten to twenty? How many no replies would you accept before you quit?

What if your good friend asks you to build her business for her? Would you carry her?

List two to three personal coping strategies for dealing with the challenges you are likely to face.

List some fun things you can do with your team to create cohesion and minimize people dropping out.

How can you keep your eyes focused on your dream until you arrive at your journey's end (financial freedom?)

CONCLUSION
OUR WISH FOR YOU

Network marketing at its best is not a get-rich-quick scheme. It's a journey of personal development toward a lifestyle of time and financial freedom that many people simply cannot imagine. As you read in the previous chapters, becoming a successful entrepreneur is a matter of dreaming big, learning a few skills, and persevering. The difference between success and quitting has nothing to do with the number of connections a person has, their sales training, or their personality. It has to do with their determination to succeed.

Is your *why* big enough? We heard a story from one of our favorite people, Jordan Adler, that illustrates this point. Imagine that you are at the top of a skyscraper in the middle of a snowstorm. Stretching out in front of you is a thin, slippery, rail-less bridge across the city. Would you cross the bridge for a hundred dollars? A thousand dollars? A million dollars?

Remember, this slippery, thin bridge is hundreds of feet above the city. The wind and snow are swirling around you. Now, imagine that your child is at the other end of that bridge, waiting to be rescued. Would you even hesitate? No matter the obstacles, you would get to your baby.

And if your why is big enough and real enough to you, you will make it through all the obstacles. You will keep going, because in the end you know it will all be worth it.

KAREN'S STORY OF PERSEVERANCE

My family and I moved from Arizona to Texas in 2010. My husband Ryan was a general contractor, and he wanted to pursue building opportunities in Texas. So, we loaded our things and began the journey to the unknown, leaving all of our friends and family behind. Not even fifteen miles out of our small Arizona town, Ryan's truck broke down. We had to be towed back, only to discover that the engine was ruined and would take weeks—and thousands of dollars—to fix. Trading in my car for a more reliable truck that would get us to Texas, we headed back on our way with only one vehicle. About ninety miles into the trip, just outside of Phoenix, we stopped for gas, only to discover that all four of the trailer's tires were losing their tread. Two hours and $500 later, we were on the road again.

When we arrived in Texas, we discovered that a flood the week before had created a run on the rental market, as a hundred families searched for temporary housing. As soon as we walked in the door of a potential property, we were told that the house was already rented. We finally found a house that would be available a month later. Fortunately, we were able to stay with some friends of my husband's parents in their one-bedroom, one-bathroom casita. (At the time, we had three children—aged three, five, and eight—and no toys or TV!)

Finally, the big moving day arrived. We loaded the kids and headed to our new home. Fifteen miles into the journey, Ryan saw something bouncing across the road in the rear-view mirror. Sure enough, we had completely lost a tire off the trailer. The wheel had broken completely off the axle.

So, late on a Sunday afternoon, we called around frantically searching for a U-Haul office that was open. We picked up the U-Haul, unpacked the trailer, loaded the U-Haul, and finally reached our destination late in the evening, exhausted but happy to finally be at the end of our journey.

A friend recently asked me, with all of that happening, how in the world did we know we were doing the right thing? She said, "We pray about things, and sometimes I think if things go smoothly, then it was meant to be. When we hit a snag, we don't push any further. I am just asking because of all the stuff that happened to try to keep you here. I am just wondering how you knew that this is what you're supposed to be doing..."

For me, the answer is that we knew why we were moving to Texas. We were certain that we were doing the right thing, and no obstacle in the world was going to stop us. Many times, just when we were about to give up hope, some little thing would show us we were on the right track.

Was our journey an easy one? NO! Was it worth it? YES! We ended up where we needed to be because we didn't give up and were certain of our destination.

OUR WISH FOR YOU

Our wish for you is that you develop yourself, work on your skills, and commit to whatever it takes to achieve your dreams. As you build your network marketing business, remember your why. We can't say it enough!
Remember how it felt to be a little girl, back when the sky was the limit, back before the worries of life bogged you down. Dream big! Let yourself soar in your imagination,

and you will soar in your life. Take this License to Dream that we are giving you today and go for it!

THE DOUBLING PENNY STORY

A wealthy father had twin teenage daughters, both of whom he thought were pretty darn sharp. One afternoon while he and his daughters sat around the kitchen table, the dad, always a firm believer in visualizing and working toward goals, offered them both a month-long apprenticeship in his business. He wanted to give them the opportunity to make enough cash to fully finance their dreams of attending major universities. In addition, the dad thought his employment offer would be a great learning experience for them.

"I've got a proposition for you! Work for me for one month in my business, and I'll pay you either $10,000 per day or a single penny on day one and double your salary every day for thirty days. I'll give a $100,000 bonus to whomever makes the most money at the end of thirty days."

Daughter #1 immediately chose the $10,000 per day option, while Daughter #2 decided to try something different and chose the doubling-penny option.

Let's put the rest of the story on hold for a moment.

Which payment option would YOU choose?

$10,000 a day or the doubling penny? Clearly, $10,000 a day adds up to $300,000. Would you choose a guaranteed

$300,000 or the unknown? Let's see if you made the right decision.

	$10, 000/day			The "Doubling Penny"	
Day	$ Paid	Total		$ Paid	Total
1	$10,000	$10,000		$.01	$.01
2	$10,000	$20,000		$.02	$.03
3	$10,000	$30,000		$.04	$.07
4	$10,000	$40,000		$.08	$.15
5	$10,000	$50,000		$.16	$.31
6	$10,000	$60,000		$.32	$.63
7	$10,000	$70,000		$.64	$1.27
8	$10,000	$80,000		$.1.28	$2.55
9	$10,000	$90,000		$2.56	$5.11
10	**$10,000**	**$100,000**		**$5.12**	**$10.23**

If you had chosen $10,000 a day, you would have earned $100,000 by the 10th day. If you had chosen the doubling penny, you would have earned only $10.23. Did you make the right choice?

Now, let's check out what happened in the next ten days...

	$10, 000/day		The "Doubling Penny"	
Day	$ Paid	Total	$ Paid	Total
11	$10,000	$110,000	$10.24	$20.47
12	$10,000	$120,000	$20.48	$40.95
13	$10,000	$130,000	$40.96	$81.91
14	$10,000	$140,000	$81.92	$163.83
15	$10,000	$150,000	$163.84	$327.67
16	$10,000	$160,000	$327.68	$655.35
17	$10,000	$170,000	$655.36	$1,310.71
18	$10,000	$180,000	$1,310.72	$2,621.43
19	$10,000	$190,000	$2,621.44	$5,242.87
20	**$10,000**	**$200,000**	**$5,242.88**	**$10,485.75**

On the 20th day, two-thirds of the month is gone. If you took the doubling penny, you would have made just over $10,000. If you had taken the $10,000 a day, you would have earned $200,000.

Only ten days left...

	$10, 000/day		The "Doubling Penny"	
Day	$ Paid	Total	$ Paid	Total
21	$10,000	$210,000	$10,485.76	$20,971.51
22	$10,000	$220,000	$20,971.52	$41,943.03
23	$10,000	$230,000	$41,943.04	$83,886.07
24	$10,000	$240,000	$83,886.08	$167,772.15
25	$10,000	$250,000	$167,772.16	$335,544.31
26	$10,000	$260,000	$335,544.32	$671,088.63
27	$10,000	$270,000	$671,088.64	$1,342,177.20
28	$10,000	$280,000	$1,342,177.20	$2,684,354.40
29	$10,000	$290,000	$2,684,354.40	$5,368,708.80
30	**$10,000**	**$300,000**	**$5,368,708.80**	**$10,737,417.00**

If you'd chosen $10,000 a day, you would have $300,000 in thirty days. But if you'd chosen the doubling penny, you would have more than TEN MILLION DOLLARS!

On the last day alone, you would have been paid more than $5 million!

This is the awesome power of compounding! When you double a small number, the result is still a small number...in the beginning. But as you continue doubling, the number gets bigger and bigger and bigger. Eventually, you achieve massive growth in a short period of time.

Look again at the chart above. If you took $10,000 a day, by the 24th day, you'd have a total of $240,000.

With the doubling penny option, your total would have been only $167,772.16. However, look at the LAST FIVE DAYS of the month—in those last five days, your doubling penny daily income grows from $167,772.16 to $5,368,708.80!

Network marketing businesses grow the same way—slowly at first. But as you keep building, the compounding effect eventually creates incredible growth. With compounding dollars, the rate of growth in this example is 100% and stays the same. The passage of time eventually creates the big numbers. With network marketing, your rate of growth actually accelerates because you are dealing with human beings, not dollars!

When you start your network marketing business, it is all about your own effort. But as you develop leaders, each of whom works to build their organization (which is a part of your organization), it is no longer only your effort. Your team's collective efforts result in "compounded compounding." Your rate of growth accelerates and your organization increases at a faster pace.

NOW, LET'S GET BACK TO THE STORY...

"You both have great minds, and I'd love for you to reach your dreams," the dad told his daughters. "However, only one of you will make enough to not only pay for college, but all of your living expenses as well. I already know who will reach that goal."

"One of you chose to be paid $10,000 a day, and I understand your decision. Most people would make the same selection. After all, $300,000 is an unheard-of amount of money for thirty days of work." The dad then turned to Daughter #2, who had chosen the penny-doubling option and said, "You took a chance and selected the doubling penny, choosing to give up the guaranteed amount without knowing how much you would be paid. Your decision to work without a guarantee has served you well. Now you can pay for your college tuition, books, lab fees, living expenses, and recreation, and still have a huge sum left over."

Daughter #2 was overjoyed! While Daughter #1 was sad that she hadn't gone with the doubling penny option, she was resilient and was able to pay all of her college expenses with the help of a part-time job. She graduated a semester later than Daughter #2.

Most people want a guaranteed salary. In network marketing, there's no guarantee. When starting up your business, it requires a lot of effort for relatively little reward, so it's common to have doubts about what you're doing. Many people give up around Day 20—right before their business is about to explode. Don't give up!

COULD YOU DO THIS?

It takes time to grow a business—any business. Compounding and teamwork allow you to grow quickly. With the right training, tools, and support, a new affiliate can bring one new team member on board every month for a year. Then you teach each new team member to do that very same thing. Let's see how your team can grow exponentially by doing this:

Month	You & Your Team Sponsor	Total Organization
1	1	2
2	1	4
3	1	8
4	1	16
5	1	32
6	1	64
7	1	128
8	1	256
9	1	512
10	1	1,024
11	1	2,048
12	1	4,096

In one year, by personally adding just one new team member each month and teaching that new member how to add one person each month, your team would grow to more than 4,000 associates! Imagine what would happen if some team members bring in more than twelve new members in a year! And what if some of them continue to bring in new people after the first year? That means greater growth and compounding, which translates into more income and faster progress toward your financial dreams and goals!

In the first six months of your business, your organization may still be relatively small. However, check out the next six months. That's when you'll really see the results of your efforts.

Of course, it will not happen exactly like this example. Some team members will do virtually nothing. Some will add less than one new person per month to the business. Some will grow your team similar to the above example.

And a few will add many, many more than one per month. (Remember the concept of the four aces?) These few will bring thousands of team members into your business and build your fortune. This is the miracle of network marketing!

ACKNOWLEDGEMENTS

JUDY O'HIGGINS

To my partners, lifelong friends, and co-authors Kristi Lee and Karen Palmer, thank you for embracing my dream. Thank you for joining me in finding a way to encourage and empower women to change their lives and get free through network marketing. Thank you for believing in my vision and for all the brilliance you brought to this book. Enrolling you in my mission was the best thing I could have done! I am a better person for knowing you, and for all you have contributed to License to Dream and to my life. It has been my great honor to work with you both, and the best is yet to come!

To John, thank you for your patience with all the hours spent on this project, for your continued support, and for believing in me all the way. I love you and will always be grateful for having you in my life. I am blessed!

To my team, who believes in me, encourages me, and inspires me every day to be my best and who builds our business with trust and integrity. You are all like family to me, and I cherish the relationships we share.

KRISTI LEE

Thank you to my dear friend Judy O'Higgins, who invited me into her dream of helping women all over the world. It has been an honor to be on this journey with you and Karen Palmer. We are just getting started in changing the world, one person at a time. You have given me one of the best gifts I could have—your friendship. Thank you for believing in me, for your support, and for traveling the world together. You have changed my life forever!

Thank you to my mom. Your unwavering belief in me and your tireless support has made it possible for me to inspire people all over the world. I love you! To my daughter Jade, for inspiring me every day to wake up with excitement for what our future looks like, and for being coachable when I teach you how to be your own boss!

Thank you to Kody and Jodi Bateman for having the courage to persevere and to lead with your hearts; you have created a company culture that is world class. Thank you to Jordan Adler for being unshakeable in your leadership and for mentoring me with visionary wisdom. Thank you to my team, many of whom have become lifelong friends, for allowing me to lead and for giving me grace when I make mistakes!

Thank you to Eric Lofholm for teaching me skills that will serve me and my team for a lifetime, and to Tom "Big Al" Schreiter for being willing to selflessly share your knowledge.

A special thank you to the leaders in our industry, who have and will selflessly teach me your skills so I can pay it forward to future generations. I appreciate you letting me stand on your shoulders!

Thank you to Jim and Leslee Testa for letting us use your beautiful car for our cover photo. We are grateful for your trust and faith in our vision for this project!

And to my Heavenly Father, for creating blessed connections and opportunities that I can serve others in your name.

KAREN PALMER

To Judy, thank you for inviting me to be a part of your vision of sharing network marketing with women. I'm so thankful and blessed to have been able to work on this project with you and Kristi. You started out as my mentors and business partners, but you have become wonderful, lifelong friends along the way. Judy, you are an inspiration to me and to everyone on your team. Thank you for believing in me.

To my husband Ryan and my kids Megan, Tristan, Josyan, and Hudson, thank you for supporting me as I spent countless hours working on this project. You are my biggest why. I love you all so much, and I wouldn't be here without you. Thank you for dreaming big with me!

Thank you to my mom and dad for always teaching me to do my best, no matter what. You instilled in me the values of hard work, commitment, and discipline, and you taught me to believe in myself.

Dad, I wish you were here to see this, but I know you're cheering me on. You always believed I could do anything. And to my stepdad Rod, thank you for believing in me and becoming an indispensable part of our family. I am so blessed to have such a tightly knit family. You may not always agree with me or "get" me, but you love me anyway and cheer me on. Thank you!

To my wonderful mother-in-law Kathy, thank you for not giving up on me and for persisting until you finally "signed me up." How great it is to have a family–in-law that loves me like their own and supports me. Thank you to you and Gary for raising incredible sons—especially the one I'm blessed to be married to.

To the amazing CEO and the phenomenal leaders in my company, who inspired me to catch the vision and dream big. Because of your coaching, I dug in my heels and made a choice to succeed. To leaders everywhere, remember that your words not only inspire people in the moment, but for a lifetime. My expanding vision has led me to places I'd never dreamed of.

Thank you for being willing to take the time to share your wisdom and belief with me and everyone else out there on this road to freedom.

Last, but certainly not least, to my Heavenly Father. Thank you for creating me in Your image, for having a plan for my life, and for creating good things for me to accomplish before I was even born. Thank you for giving me the desires of my heart and the courage to believe they are possible.

ABOUT THE AUTHORS

JUDY O'HIGGINS

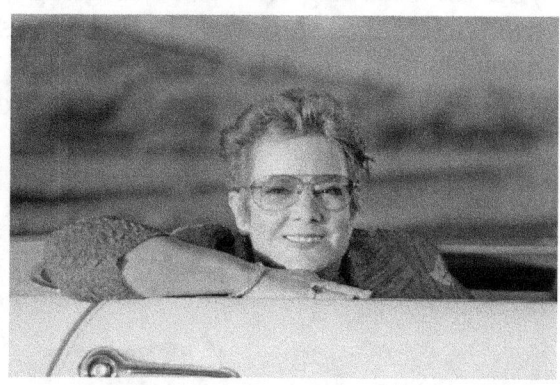

Judy O'Higgins was raised in Connecticut, but made her way west after graduating from the University of Michigan School of Social Work with an MSW and serving for two years in VISTA (the domestic Peace Corps) in the 1960s. She lived in San Diego for many years, but migrated to Arizona to become a homeowner with land, a garden, and various animals, including chickens, goats, a horse, dogs, and a cat.

Judy ran a thirty-day recovery program for substance abusers in Sedona, AZ for four years. That was her last job working for someone else. In 1990, she opened a private counseling practice and became a solopreneur, helping hundreds of women to overcome negative programming and empower themselves to better relationships, jobs, self-esteem, and family functionality. Her greatest love was helping women to believe in themselves and to do things they didn't think were possible.

Judy was introduced to network marketing in 1996 and instantly loved the concept of working with teams in a win-win environment for the common goal of financial freedom. Her first company failed, temporarily ending Judy's dream of retiring with residual income for life. Now she knows that was just practice for her second company, where she has risen to be in the top twenty-five distributors and created enough monthly residual income to retire from her counseling career after just two years.

Judy is still helping empower women to a better life by believing in themselves, doing things they didn't think were possible, getting their dreams back, and creating financial freedom for themselves and their families through network marketing. Her goals include national and worldwide travel as her company expands internationally to spread the concept of residual income through network marketing to women worldwide. She encourages every woman to dream big, work hard, and see the job through to the reap the rewards of freedom and a family legacy of generational wealth.

KRISTI LEE

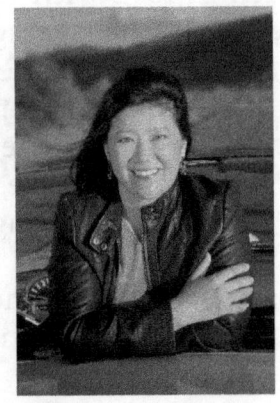

Kristi Lee was born and raised in Los Angeles, California, the youngest of three girls in a second-generation Chinese family. Kristi was taught growing up that success meant graduating from college and getting a traditional nine-to-five job. She graduated college with a Bachelor of Science degree in business administration and worked in the corporate world in marketing and retail for twenty years. Her responsibilities included category management, sales growth, and advertising for health and beauty products for 2,300 retail stores across the U.S.

Kristi's corporate career involved multiple moves to different states. In 1999, she was again told she was going to be moved—this time to Boise, Idaho. She had a feeling the company was not making the move for the right reasons, and she walked away from her twenty-three-year career. Seven months later, after most of her colleagues had made the move, the company announced it was for sale, stranding many of her friends in Boise where the job market was not robust and the housing market was going to see a flood of For Sale signs. It was then that she realized she never wanted to work for a company where she had a boss, and she vowed she would help as many people have choices about being free—from job stress, financial debt, and too much time away from their families.

Her first experience with network marketing was negative. When she was a young child, family members on her father's side were involved in a company that would never reveal their name until they tricked you into attending one of their opportunity meetings. Kristi was reintroduced to network marketing in 2006, while going through a divorce and having her corporate job move out of state. Once she fell in love with her company's product and service, and the idea of leveraging time, she left the corporate world behind and has never looked back.

Kristi taught her then-three-year-old daughter Jade, who was very shy, the importance of lifelong skills: looking people in the eye, shaking hands, having conversations, and understanding that there are so many options other than a traditional corporate job. She has a passion for inspiring women and children to step into their power and share their gifts and talents with the world.

KAREN PALMER

Born and raised in Arizona, Karen Palmer grew up in the small town of Camp Verde. In 1995, Karen left Camp Verde to attend college, marrying her high-school sweetheart Ryan in 1996. After graduating from Northern Arizona University with a BA in English in 1998 and a MA in Rhetoric in 2000, Karen and Ryan moved to Phoenix, where 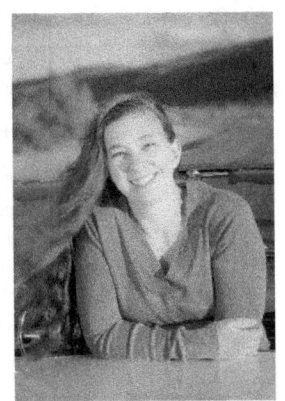 Karen was an English professor at Grand Canyon University.

In 2002, their first child, a beautiful baby girl, was born. Desiring to raise their children in the small-town atmosphere they loved, the Palmers moved back to Camp Verde, where Ryan began a thriving contracting business building custom homes. Over the next few years, Ryan and Karen added two handsome boys to their young family, and Karen spent her days taking care of their home, helping Ryan in his business, and homeschooling their kids.

However, in 2008, Karen saw her life of being a stay-at-home mom jeopardized by the failing economy. Together with her husband Ryan, Karen decided to take a leap of faith. She began building a network marketing business that would enable her to stay home with her kids and protect their family from the market downturn. For Karen, network marketing was a source of hope in those trying times, and her business provided her family with much-needed additional income.

More importantly, in building her business, Karen learned to dream big. Over the past fifteen years, she has seen many of her dreams fulfilled, including publishing two books, earning her PhD, and adding a fourth little one to the family in 2016! The skills that she learned as a network marketing professional have served her well in all aspects of her life, as Karen has taken on multiple leadership roles in her community. Today, Karen lives in a renovated 100-year-old farmhouse on a mini-farm with her family, a pair of mini zebus, a Great Pyrenees, an orange tabby, and what often feels like a million chickens. She is an English Professor at Yavapai College in Prescott, Arizona.

www.ingramcontent.com/pod-product-compliance
Lightning Source LLC
Chambersburg PA
CBHW070754220526
45467CB00014B/314